Exploring Whitchurch History

growth of a Shropshire town

Paul Anderton

with members and friends of Whitchurch History and Archaeology Group

Jean North, Joan Barton, Sue Cleaves, Maude Gould, Lindsay Green, Janet Miller, Mary Perry, June Potter and Kathleen Priddy

Copyright Paul Anderton 2009

All rights reserved. No part of this publication may be reproduced, stored in a retrieval system, transmitted in any form by any means electrical or mechanical, photographed, recorded or otherwise without the prior permission of the publisher.

Published 2009

Published by Whitchurch History and Archaeology Group, Shropshire

Printed by Delmar Press (Colour Printers) Ltd, Wall Lane, Nantwich, Cheshire CW5 5LS

ISBN : 978-0-9564059-0-6

Contents

	Page
Exploring the history of Whitchurch	1
Maps and Plans	3
Whitchurch today	5
Whitchurch the town: successive stages in expansion to 1918	9
The town to 1761	
The town to 1859	
Victorian improvements	
Jubilee Park	
The Salisbury Road area : an Edwardian suburb	19
West End and Chemistry	25
Local Authority housing 1918 –1952	30
William Fowler and seventeenth century maps	43
Whitchurch people in the 1630s	57
The plague in Whitchurch 1650-51	62
The Duke of Bridgewater's estates in Whitchurch 1761	67
Whitchurch mills	75
Black Park farms 1761-1839 and a field survey 1814	81
Whitchurch about 1840: explorations using tithe maps	87
Whitchurch markets	94
1910 Land Valuation Survey	107
Last thought – a look towards the future	120

Acknowledgements

Interest in the subjects explored in this book grew out of classes in Whitchurch led by Paul Anderton for Keele University Continuing and Professional Education Centre in parallel with other classes directed by Madge Moran. The first debt, therefore, is owed to all those who attended on so many Tuesday mornings to learn about and to contribute to a history of Whitchurch. Several members voluntarily continued to work on the approach to discovering history adopted in this book, and the joint efforts of Joan Barton, Sue Cleaves, Maude Gould, Lindsay Green, Janet Miller, Mary Perry, June Potter and Kathleen Priddy have ensured that new light can now be thrown on the way Whitchurch has developed over the ages. Jean North is especially thanked not only for her contribution to the group, but also because without her skill and patience as a mapmaker this book could not exist. Sincere thanks are due to Joan Barton for her generous contributions to the work of the Classes and the warm encouragement she has given over many years to all those interested in the history of Whitchurch. Joan's previous work on the theme of plague in the 1650s is the basis of one of the following chapters. Maude Gould researched the struggle to achieve market reform in the 1870s to make another chapter possible. Individuals in the group have learned much from Madge Moran, and more recently from Dr. Fran Bumpus, and they too are thanked for their input, however indirectly made. Dr. Anne Tarver is gratefully acknowledged for work digitising the map summarising the physical expansion of Whitchurch.

Much research was conducted in Shropshire Archives where the Search Room staff were always graciously helpful. Grateful thanks are due to the Archivist, Mary Mackenzie, and to Helen Haynes, for assistance with the reproduction of, and permission on behalf of the Archives to publish, the following documents: referenced as follows : on the cover and page 13 (380/34/Bundle 489), page 30 Gas Agreement (DA15/743/17), page 36 watercolour 6001/1236, page 39 Smallbrook plan (DA15/135/28/1-5), page 44 Fowler signature (212/Box 466/18), page 51 AS maps including Tilstock (212/Box 466/6), page 53 AS map of Blackoe (212/Box 466/9), page 71 two maps from G.Grey's Book (212/479/3-4), page 100 election poster (2794/Box 23). Extracts from probate inventories (pages 2 and 45) are reproduced by kind permission of Lichfield Record Office. Trevor Rowley is thanked for permission to use his sketch plan on page 55, and A.D.M.Phillips for the cartouche page 4. Ordnance Survey maps on pages 3, 19, 31 and 113 are acknowledged as Crown Copyright. Mr Ray Grocott is thanked for the photographs from his collection. It has not been possible to trace the source of photographs taken out of the Whitchurch History and Archaeology Group's Collection so that sincere apologies are given if permission to reproduce has inadvertently not been obtained.

Whitchurch History and Archaeology Group are very grateful indeed for the financial assistance given by the Owen Family Trust, the Walker Trust and Grocontinental to enable the publication of this work at the standard desired.

This book includes only a small part of the findings of the research group, and it leaves open many possibilities for further inquiries and publications.

EXPLORING THE HISTORY OF WHITCHURCH

The story of Whitchurch can be told in many ways and there are scores of chapters that could be included. Some of the more unusual subjects are explored in this book.

The idea is to contribute to an explanation of how Whitchurch has come to be what it is today. Maps feature a lot because they are what explorers use. Some are old maps and vital sources of information, some are specially drawn to present discoveries visually. The purpose of going to new territories is to plot the landscape: here timescale is just as important.

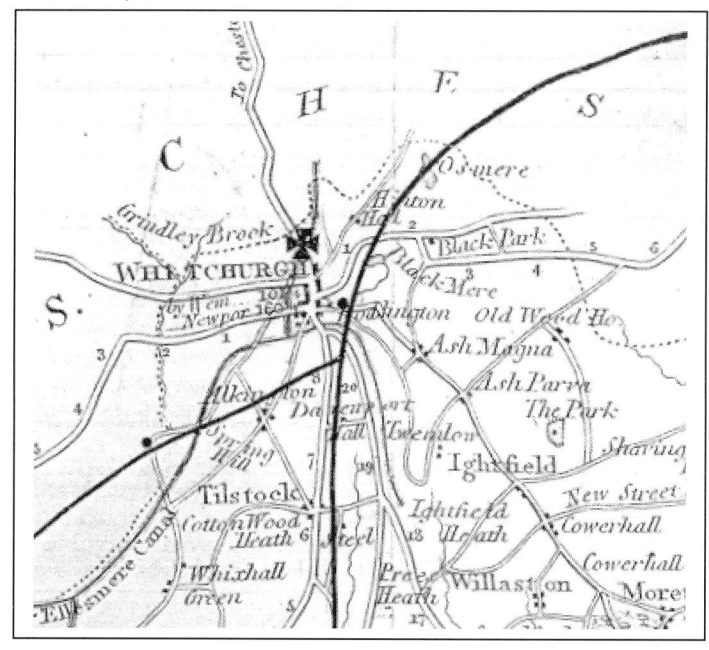

Exploring the past involves studying many other sorts of evidence, not the least being piles of manuscripts and printed documents. They are the landmarks which pioneers use as guides to find their way around previous, unfamiliar and puzzling times. They need to be read and understood, related one to another and explained to all those who want to learn about the history of their families and communities – and perhaps become explorers themselves. Just as maps are prominent in the stories which follow, so are the documentary sources which give them substance.

History is never final and complete. Inquiries into the past, even for Whitchurch, never reveal all that can be said. Each is conducted for a particular reason and liable to be partial in every sense; all explorers set out from different points in time and are shaped by different social, political and economic circumstances. This book does not attempt to provide a chronological or comprehensive narrative from beginning to end. The date at which this exploration sets out is that of the time of producing the first surviving maps, and the lifetime of the first known mapmaker, William Fowler. The intention is deliberately to explore a territory in different directions and within limits of space and time to provoke and encourage others to make more journeys into the same past. They should also have similarly varied sources openly acknowledged. Maps are prominent here; census records, probate inventories, a box of family letters, or minute books and membership lists of sports clubs could equally be starting points for different explorations of previous ages. In this way a richer history of Whitchurch is accumulated.

Taken together, these present studies should give readers further knowledge about one Shropshire town and a greater understanding of a historical process of change which applies to many other English communities. True, the three hundred years of change considered here understates the importance of the thousand years which came before. The premise on which all is based, however, is the condition of Whitchurch today – a town far from unusual in the kaleidoscope of England's landscape. How has it arrived at this condition? This is the million pound question.

By no means all the answers can be found in the last three hundred years, nor locally. The town has never been detached from change across the British Isles in general, or from movements affecting Europe as a whole. This book has to assume in the reader some understanding of these longer, wider processes which have pressed heavily on the town's development. The history of Whitchurch is just as much unique and individual as it is a vivid and close-up demonstration of the general. It's enough of a task just to deal with the transformation of the town from that which William Fowler knew in 1650 to that seen today. To find out more about William Fowler and changes since his day, read on!

Whitchurch Maps and Plans

The first maps which inspired these inquiries were drawn in the seventeenth century. One of the surveyors can be named – William Fowler – but others are unknown. In fact, little has been found out about any of the men who drew maps and plans of Whitchurch. George Grey was employed to plot the town and surrounding hamlets in the mid-eighteenth century, but the people who worked for the Ordnance Survey Office in the nineteenth century are anonymous. For the most part, all the drawings have to be taken at face value and considered without access to the instructions given to the surveyors, or their life stories.

The range of materials available for Whitchurch history goes, for example, from a coloured, unscaled and semi-pictorial representation of the course of Stags Brook flowing out of Blakemere, through the town and out westwards to Red Brook, to current editions of Ordnance Survey Landranger maps. It includes plans of mill pools, farms, housing estates and individual dwellings. County maps have not been ignored, as for instance that by John Roque in 1752 and Bacon's new survey of Staffordshire and Shropshire in the 1920s. By no means all of the possible records have been seen for present purposes, but the selection highlights the richness of map sources from which local historians can acquire considerable amounts of information.

Maps present unique data and display visually information almost impossible to understand in any other way. They show distributions across space and relative locations

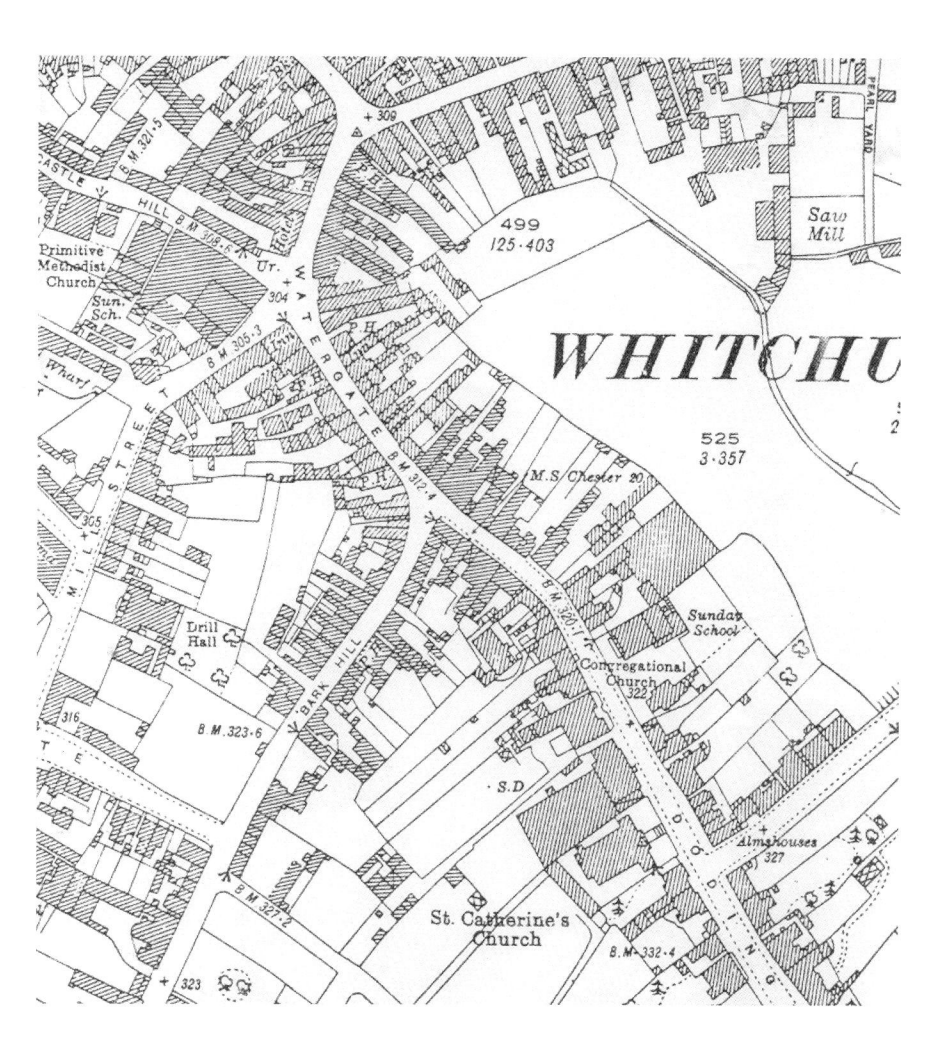

Ordnance Survey map 1926
Crown copyright

immediately recognisable. Each separately conveys a good deal of basic information, but it is the possibilities of putting drawings alongside one another to arrive at comparative conclusions about, for example, changes taking place over time which interest the local historian.

William Fowler's maps of 1650 and George Grey's surveys of 1761 are of great significance when studied in this way. They can then be compared with later maps such as those made for the Tithe Award 1837-42 and the Inland Revenue Valuations maps 1910-14. From the 1860s onwards, local map makers had the national surveys of the Ordnance Survey Office to call on which might explain the basis for a map of the town dated 1859, and certainly provided the plans included in estate sale catalogues of 1920.

Plans of small parts of Whitchurch abound. One particularly valuable collection, investigated in part at least for inquiries into the twentieth century expansion of Whitchurch town, is that relating to the building of houses by Whitchurch Urban District Council. There is a much fuller history to be written about the role of local government in housing provision than is provided here. A major gap is also the absence of explanation of private house building and commercial and industrial constructions which is the consequence of sources being widely scattered, if they exist at all.

Maps have to be interpreted; their full import is not always immediately obvious, and they can mislead. They have to be placed in a context derived from all other written evidence – indeed from field observations and surviving artefacts as well. Quite possibly not all the information which can be squeezed out of the maps and plans consulted here is presented in the following accounts.

Local historians of Whitchurch should see the importance of maps for their researches, however, after reading these reports of explorations into Whitchurch history inspired by maps.

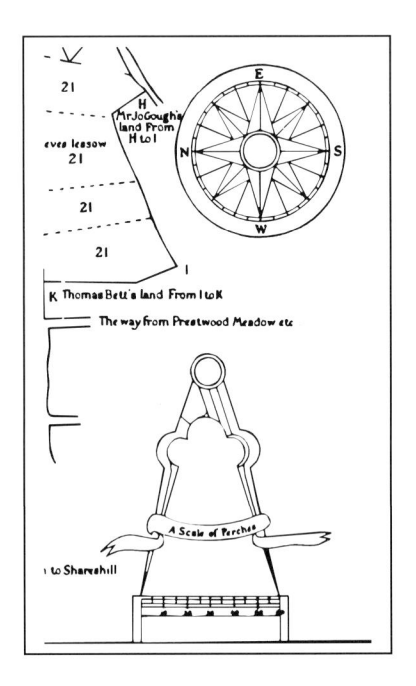

Above
Detail from a copy by A.D.M. Phillips of a map of Prestwood Farm near Wolverhampton surveyed by William Fowler May 1661

Whitchurch today

People living in Whitchurch today are watching its character change. Some with long memories say quite easily that it's now a dormitory town without work. Others still look at it as a small country town with a market on Fridays to prove it. They admit though that they can see unwelcome signs of a different town developing. 'So many houses have been built lately', they say, 'that's altered how Whitchurch was'.

Visitors walking along Green End and up High Street soon have a sense of history. Here buildings are obviously long established: old in fact. Hardly surprising that 'Old – but not old fashioned' became a tourist office slogan. There's some truth in it. New fashions in private housing estates and super-stores increasingly show up among the Victorian and Edwardian buildings just outside the narrow central core of the medieval town. Inevitably, opinions vary as to the effect on the community of new retail stores and a commuter life-style. Some see Tesco as among the worst features of the town: others find it a natural meeting place. In-comers comment favourably on the friendliness of the place, but the young find much of their entertainment elsewhere. Of course, Whitchurch is hardly exceptional among English towns in having to respond to the technologies and social change of a wider global economy. It is, nevertheless, a distinctive place with recognisable features that have grown over time past. They define the community to which residents are happy to say they belong.

For administrative purposes it's one of four urban areas within the North Shropshire District Authority. The headquarters are in Wem. The town is divided between three of the Authority's electoral wards. The Census of 2001 reported 8,815 people in Whitchurch, or just over 15% of those living within the North Shropshire Local Authority. There is a lingering feeling of regret that the town no longer has its own all-embracing local government body. Sharing a District Council with Market Drayton, Ellesmere and Wem is a blow to civic pride – a feeling common in the other communities no doubt since the amalgamation in 1974.

The separation of town and country is fairly sharp: there is little urban sprawl or straggling ribbons of housing along main roads leading out of town. Whitchurch has been, and still is, a somewhat self-contained community although serving as the social centre for a wide surrounding rural area. There's a lot of comfort found in a claim made in the first years of the twenty-first century that the North Shropshire area is among the top ten best places to live in England.

A very obvious feature of its layout now is the by-pass road which relieves the historic heart of destructive lorries. Of course, it could itself become a magnetic attraction for commercial investment. It's a reminder that Whitchurch was born alongside and grew up serving a major routeway from North Wales and Chester to Shrewsbury and London. Roads are likely to remain crucial to the town's continuing prosperity.

Many of the economic features found in other ancient Shropshire towns are shared by Whitchurch, not least that of being home to commuters using cars. It retains some of its traditional shopping trade but super-markets loom large. The iron works has gone, and J.B.Joyce & Co., clockmakers, do little by way of manufacturing in the town. The firm claims origins in the late seventeenth century, but is now part of the Smith Group. What Whitchurch does have, however, and it's very much in the tradition of the town, is one of Britain's most prestigious road transport businesses. Grocontinental started as a family business in the 1920s and under the guidance of Ray Grocott, and more recently Linda and David his daughter and son, the firm has expanded into a massive haulage and storage business with something like one hundred trailers travelling widely in Britain and Europe. In 2004 it was recognised as Motor Transport's Haulier of the Year, and Shropshire's Business of the Year.

Census 2001: Population			
Whitchurch Wards	Population	% under 16yrs	% over 60 yrs
North	2714	16.6	26.4
West	3144	20.8	22.4
South	2957	21.1	24.3
	8815		
North Shropshire totals	57,108	19.4	23.4
England & Wales totals		20.2	20.9

For Whitchurch the presence of this business with an international reputation is an economic bonus. Grocontinental not only provides employment for over 250 people but has major links with other large firms in North Shropshire such as Müller at Market Drayton. The account of business development which Ray Grocott provides in his contribution to the book *Wheels of Fortune* is most instructive as to the part played by a family business in the local economy today.

In the dairy farming region around, for which the town has long served as a market centre, cheese-making and liquid milk for other dairy products are still important, but only a handful of farms lie within the three electoral wards which define the town. Four solicitors' offices, three dental surgeons, and eight bank or building society branches are among the more important services located in the main streets.

One way to sum up the nature of Whitchurch today is to quote its website as of July 2007. 'Today work is found in manufacturing, agriculture, construction, catering, tourism, banking & finance, transport and services as well as many small businesses and self-employed occupations. Three new housing estates are currently under construction and new businesses continue to open and grow (there are four local industrial estates). The Town has all the modern requirements of a retail centre, a railway station and a town paper, the *Whitchurch Herald*, which comes out every Thursday.'

Commerce isn't the only important feature of the town. The Community Hospital, for example, is associated with three GP practices and is the focus of much local pride. There is a real feeling that but for a vociferous campaign organised within the town this would have been removed by central government. Indeed, one of the ways in which the distinctiveness of a place is marked out is by the strength of unifying bonds not apparent until some threat is made to a local service. The community may well gain strength also from needing but one secondary school – two could split loyalties. On the other hand, it's a pity it isn't large enough to have more than an outpost of the North Shropshire College for further education purposes.

In an age of television and electronic communication the town's social and cultural characteristics are not much different from many other places. For those with space between school, work and travel, on the one hand, and television and internet surfing on the other, there is a possibility for socialising in the town's rugby, hockey and cricket clubs, church meetings, amateur dramatic societies and pubs. Among team sports rugby commands the most attention: the club has a well-established reputation for the hospitality offered to visiting teams. The extent to which the town's residents do support these voluntary associations, and the other amenities such as the library, Civic Centre and Heritage Centre, is difficult to measure. However, this is the way that loyalty to a local community is expressed, and the means by which the distinctiveness of Whitchurch is retained in a world of mass entertainment and a homogeneous culture.

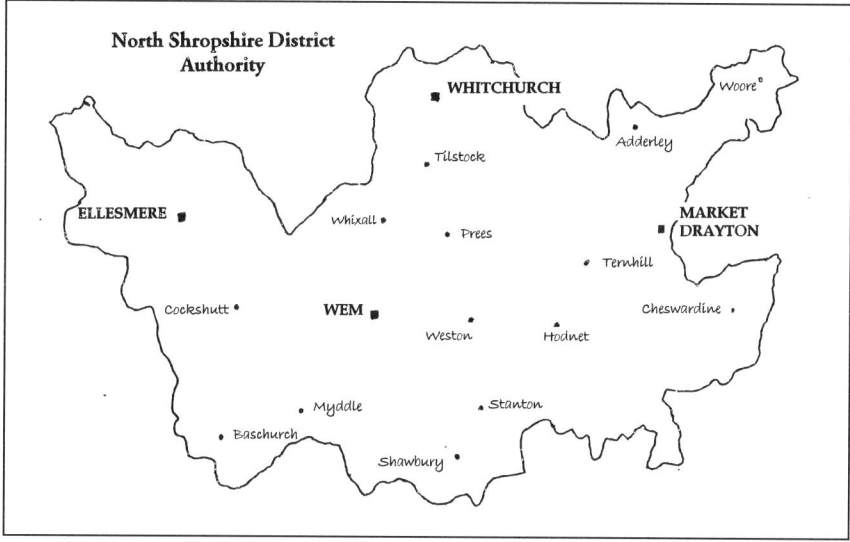

The past …

… reflected in the present

From medieval street pattern and renowned industries, war sacrifices and rebuilt Civic Centre

to private housing estates and four men with 140 years service in one company

Whitchurch town: successive stages in expansion to 1918

What can be seen at present in Whitchurch is the latest stage of growth. An explorer of history needs maps to explain how this has come about. A close look at a succession of plans shows the nature, speed and extent of alteration over time. Fortunately, among the numerous maps of various parts of the district from 1651 onwards there is a series of town plans available for comparison.

The earliest known plan of Whitchurch town dates from 1761. This was done by George Grey for the Duke of Bridgewater as part of a survey of lands he owned in North Shropshire. The Duke was starting a career as a promoter and financial backer of canals. He needed to know just what he was worth, and George Grey, from Lancaster, was instructed to map and report on the manor of Whitchurch. A few of the buildings Grey plotted in the town were differentiated by distinctive shading, and numbered in a schedule. These properties were leased out at rents or on terms valuable to the Duke's estate. Houses in Pepper Alley and two large buildings on the east side of High Street, just south of Church Lane, were among them. The vast majority of the properties, however, were carefully marked out, but not numbered nor were their occupiers named. They were copyhold plots bringing in negligible revenue by that date from rents or feudal dues.

Street names had been in use for two or more centuries. Their layout had not substantially changed so the basic medieval linear plan of the town can be reconstructed. No attempt is made here to examine the relationship to the Roman fort over which the Saxon settlement spread. Sufficient to say that the site of St. Alkmund's church and the routeway against which it was built, with the dwellings constructed either side of the road which took the name High Street, formed the spine of a linear settlement. Two streets at right angles led eastwards, one starting as Church Street then extended into Claypit Street, and the other got the name Green End. Successive stages in the subsequent expansion of the town are somewhat arbitrary, but Grey's map provides a convenient marker.

The town to 1761

A traveller from the north came first to Bargates, which name is almost self-explanatory as an entrance through a wall, or gated lane (yate meaning lane), and then arrived at

Bargates about 1900

the church of St. Alkmund. From there, downhill, was High Street, to the Bull Ring, after which a stream had to be crossed in Watergate, before a long, slow climb along Dodington was necessary to leave the town at its southern exit. Parallel to the east side of High Street, at the back of houses and long gardens, there developed the appropriately named Back Street (St. Mary's Street) with gardens stretching further east to open country. Access to this, at a right angle, at its northern end was by Church Lane which continued beyond as St. Luke's Street (otherwise The Nooke or Claypit Street). At the southern end of Back Street another right angle led into St. John's Street, and out to fields. This deviated, however, on the way west into High Street, with a pronounced kink. The other major street at right angles to High Street, coming out of the Bull Ring, was Green End which was the principal route into the town from its eastern side.

People coming from Wales almost certainly approached Whitchurch up Sherra Hill (Sherrymill Hill) and reached Bargates inside the line of any wall, on a street called Yardington. A castle once stood on the crest of the hill south of this area, but between Yardington and the street called Castle Hill the district came to be known as Newtown by 1601 at the latest.[1] In effect, Newtown was to houses on the west side of High Street what Back Street was to those on the east – the rear point of entry. Properties in Newtown had gardens which dropped steeply down the scarp slope. The name is almost certainly evidence that here was the first significant expansion of the medieval road-side settlement of Whitchurch.

There was possibly a spurt of growth again in the early seventeenth century, but other than in Newtown and by way of in-filling on High Street and in Back Street, it would seem that the pattern of new settlement was ribbon

High Street and St. Alkmund's about 1910

development along existing streets. Green End and Dodington were probably the most attractive sites, but there was some construction in Claypit Street. The 1761 plan shows the limits reached on the eve of a new communications age when canals and turnpike roads made a considerable impact elsewhere on urban expansion. It shows the Bark Hill area, where the trackway from Alkington entered Dodington, as perhaps the spot for building which most intrigues. It would seem that there were already houses on what would become Scotland Street and others in Rosemary Lane. When eventually a canal branch arrived in Whitchurch in 1811 it stopped close by. No doubt this helped to determine a new street pattern which is evident on the 1859 map made for Earl Brownlow to show the properties he inherited from the Bridgewater estate.

1761 George Grey's plan of the urban settlement.

The north-south alignment of the town on two sides of the routeway that was the origin of its existence is very clear. Development north of the church was probably constricted by glebe lands over which successive rectors had control.

Expansion west was hindered by the steep slope down which fell narrow strips of gardens from dwellings in Newtown. Stags Brook flowed across the main road at Watergate from a pool and marshy area to the east which was unsuitable for house building. Ribbons of cottages interspersed with imposing houses lined both sides of Dodington as the road stretching away to the south became known.

Green End attracted development where roads from Nantwich and Market Drayton came in from the east to a junction not shown here. Claypit Street was another promising district for new building by 1761.

Pepper Street was an important link between High Street and Newtown. This and the district immediately to the south was heavily congested by 1761.

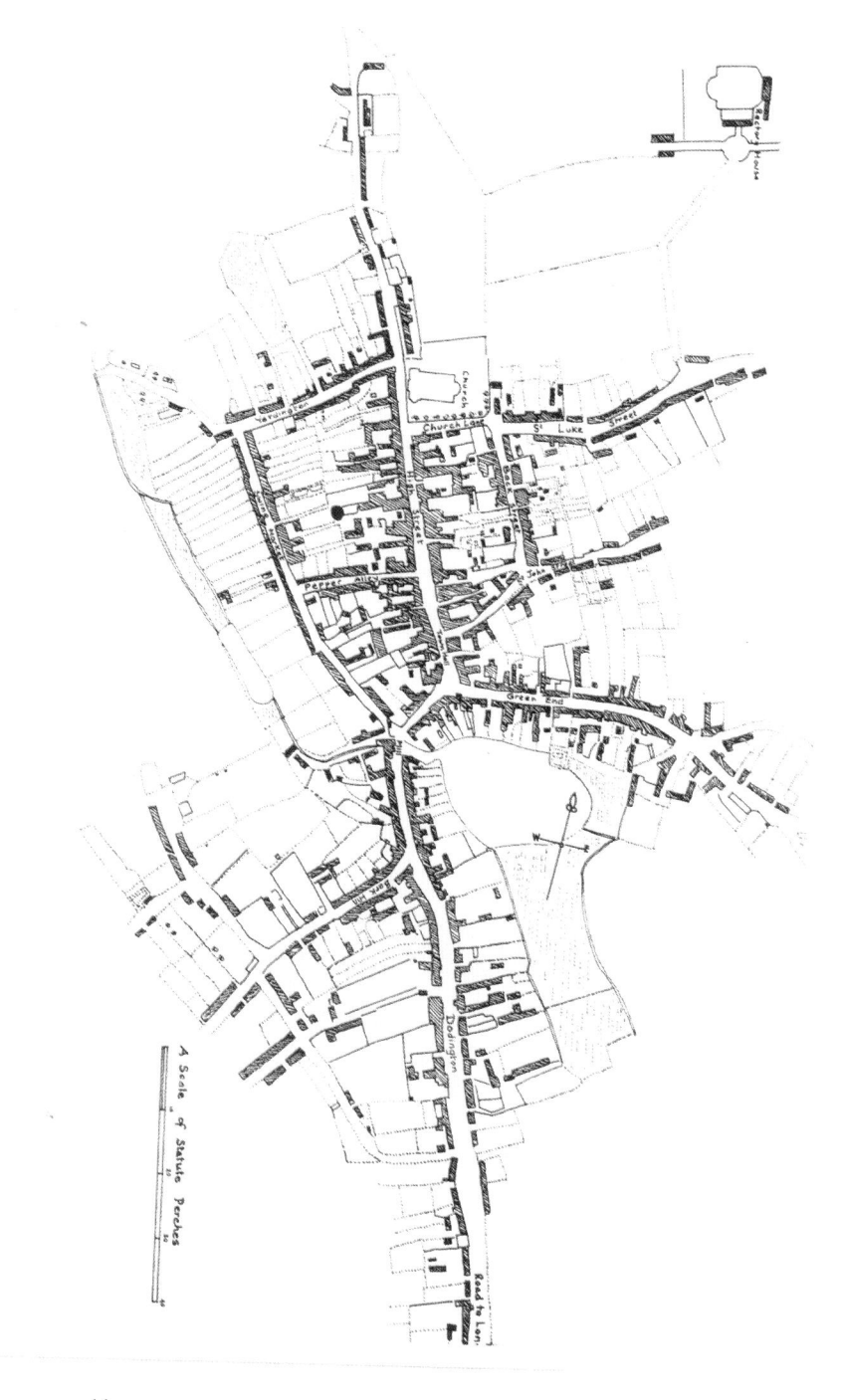

The town by 1859

Plans to provide Whitchurch with a canal link to the outside world were under discussion in the 1790s. Actual construction met with some resistance, but the branch from the main Ellesmere Canal Company's cut followed a course parallel to Stags Brook to a wharf almost adjacent to the old town mill. The 1859 map shows the site quite plainly. Mill Street was opened up in 1811 to link Watergate Street to the wharf and was called originally New Street. It was then extended by New Road to shorten the route out to Wrexham.

The economic effect of the canal dug rather late in the development of these artificial waterways is difficult to isolate on the evidence of maps alone. There is no sign in 1859 of buildings on the wharf site or of a corn mill a few yards long the canal on its opposite bank – both appear on the 1880 Ordnance Survey 25 inches to the mile edition. Another commercial development in this area possibly owing something to the availability of water transport was a large dairy just beyond Scotland Street. This too, however, was erected after 1859 but before 1880.

Highgate and Scotland Street appear to be more heavily developed by 1859. Incidentally, Scotland Street has reverted to its eighteenth century name, taken from the field in which it was built. In 1859 it is marked as Havannah Buildings because it incorporated some cottages erected by Joseph Hassall who died in 1829. He was a banker who had significant interests in Liverpool shipping. He was credited with completing a frigate for the Royal Navy during the wars with France after 1803 when the original contractors failed. This ship was called *The Havannah,* perhaps commemorating a famous siege and battle in 1762 when British troops occupied Cuba. The launch of this vessel greatly pleased Liverpool merchants and enhanced the Whitchurch man's reputation. Hassall's eleven dwellings were an addition to 25 properties in Scotland Lane according to the Whitchurch Rate Book 1827.[2] Unfortunately, Hassall died a bankrupt.

The most impressive new feature of the 1859 map is the Union Workhouse, originally the House of Industry, erected in the 1790s.[3] This was testimony to a notable alteration in social welfare provision in the parish. In some ways it anticipated the national reform of poor law operations instituted in 1834. Its existence certainly kept the parish out of the wholesale reorganisation of poor law authorities carried out in the late 1830s. It also meant that when union with other parishes became inevitable in 1854 it was this workhouse which was the central institution. Had the powers-that-be had their way in 1836 Whitchurch would have been subordinate to Ellesmere!

The physical expansion of Whitchurch between 1761 and 1859, in other words, was almost entirely contained within the former limits with only small extensions of the ribbons of Green End, Claypit Street and Sherrymill Hill. This last road crossed the canal and a Gas Works was erected at this point in 1826 by Messrs Edwards and Smith to supply street lighting. Finally, a small settlement had begun on the Chester Road, with The Mount as the principal house. Of course, this confinement within long established limits meant a heavier concentration of population and buildings in an already built-up area creating an environment increasingly seen as deleterious to health and prosperity. Whitchurch was far from unusual in this form of development and neither was it alone among towns with grossly inadequate governing authorities quite unable to deal with social problems.

1859 Map for Earl Brownlow

This identified property within the Brownlow estate which the Earl inherited from the Bridgewaters. The map maker and the basis for his survey are uncertain, but as the whole town was plotted it allows for direct comparisons with Grey's earlier plan and later Ordnance Survey maps.

Victorian improvements

Between 1859 and 1880 a significant alteration in the pattern of streets took place. Dodington was linked to Claypit Street by the construction of Bridgewater Street and Brownlow Street. This almost looks like an eastern by-pass for the town and it opened up the territory between the old town and its most recent communications link – the railway. It was not a convenient way of avoiding the bottlenecks of Bargates and High Street, however, because the necessary link across Claypit Street to the Chester Road, north of Bargates, was not possible at this time. It would have crossed through Rectory land. The new road required some removal of properties around the point where a Police Station had been erected in 1860. This was close to the division of Green End into two lanes, one known as Tin Hole Lane, which had been the trackway to Waymills, and the other called Paradise Street and the start of the ancient road to Combermere and Nantwich. These were respectively renamed Station Road, for the obvious reason that it had become a significant route when the railway was opened in 1858, and Talbot Street. A large junction was the result at the centre of which a fountain was placed in 1882. In effect, the construction of the arc of roads to the east of the ancient settlement created the opportunity to build a new suburb of improved housing.

The scale of this Bridgewater-Brownlow street project, completed in 1877, is evidence of a mid-Victorian interest in re-developing Whitchurch and making necessary improvements. In consequence, it became possible to remove cattle sales on market days from the crowded Watergate and Castle Hill streets to a new Smithfield fronting on to Brownlow Street. This was opened in November 1878.

Left : *Brownlow Street*   Right : *Police Station, both 2007*

It was no accident that these major changes in the layout of the town followed the creation in 1860 of a new public authority, the Local Sanitary Board. The express purpose of Parliament in setting up these Boards, elected by ratepayers, was to ensure that sufficient powers were exercised locally to clean up streets, supply fresh water, drain away sewage and remove 'nuisances' considered dangerous to health. One major obstacle to environmental improvement, in many towns as well as Whitchurch, was that the right to hold and control markets of all kinds was in private hands. Whitchurch was especially handicapped as there was not even an Improvement Commission for the town.

Above: *Smithfield Market about 1939*

Left: *An impression of the new cattle market shortly after opening 1878*

Whitchurch elected its first Board in March 1861 but it was years before it began serious planning to fulfil its obligations. In 1869 the issue of better facilities for the sale of food – in practice, an indoor market – and the related problem of removing animals for sale from the streets on market days – in other words, a separate Cattle Market – at last came to the top of the Board's agenda. The editor of the newly founded

Whitchurch Herald commented on this progress :

The Local Board and committee in connection with the same, have thus shown that they intend to have the town provided with a Market-Hall: and we doubt not that there will be other improvements in connection with it. This is a move in the right direction. We see other towns, not near so important as our own, moving with the times, and why should we then be at a standstill with regard to improvements? We notice in the world a few who would always remain in status quo, and who fancy every step taken in the way of advancement will be the cause of injuring their trade, and who are afraid that interlopers will come in and take the profit which they as ratepayers ought to have. How long is this state of narrow-mindedness to last in the enlightened age in which we live?' [4]

The editor was correct in anticipating that a chain of improvements had to take place just to get a new Market Hall and Smithfield, and the list did not end when these facilities opened. The demand for fresh water had still to be satisfied, for example, but at least there was movement where formerly there had been none

The Wesleyan Methodists took advantage of change and built a new chapel, called St. John's Church, immediately to the north of Smithfield, which they opened in 1879. Just across Brownlow Street from the chapel, a Cottage Hospital was erected in 1886, having been under discussion for at least two years. Another community facility, Public Bathhouse, was put up also on Brownlow Street, close to Talbot Street, in 1891. In 1900 a new Fire Station was erected almost adjacent to the baths.

Attention shifted from this eastern district in the later Victorian period. Land across the canal jumped into prominence for reasons not immediately generated locally.

Top : *The Manse for St. John's Wesleyan Methodist Church seen in 2007*
Below : *Public Baths 1891 as photographed in 2007*

Jubilee Park

On the other side of town from Brownlow Street there was little change until Queen Victoria celebrated her Golden Jubilee in 1887. A public meeting in February supported festivities in Whitchurch for this occasion, but there were moves to make a more permanent memorial of the Queen's achievement. Public disagreements marred the selection of a project because there was a strong body of opinion in favour of building swimming baths that was ignored by the select group who formed themselves into a committee to make the arrangements.

Particular members of the committee who favoured opening a recreation ground or public park then purchased over eleven acres of land alongside the canal. This was, in fact, used for children's sports on the day of the Jubilee celebration in June. The money came from a public appeal to which just over 100 people were advertised as making contributions. Mrs Nottingham, with £500, Major Lee and Mr Beck, with £100 each, were the largest donors and were suspected by some of influencing the committee to drop the baths scheme and buy land for a park instead. In effect, the owners of the Jubilee Field became a trust which turned agricultural land into a place for relaxation and pleasurable exercise open to all. They used £1,250 of the £1,450 or so raised by the appeal to buy the land and thus had little left over for any kind of landscaping and maintenance. They had, in any case, to spend about £200 on sports and feasting on 25 June when the townspeople had a day off work. [5]

A substantial area on the west side of the town thus became unavailable for building. Not only this, but it was not properly developed for recreation purposes either. In fact, when the Queen reached her next landmark in 1897 there was still resentment at the betrayal of public demand ten years earlier, and one of the principal proposals to commemorate the Diamond Jubilee was for the very recently established Urban District Council to take over the Trust and complete the park project b,y among other things, providing a proper entrance. The alternative was an extension to the Cottage Hospital (baths had been built in 1891). Both ways of marking the occasion were adopted as a compromise and the park was transferred to the Urban District Council. It was a couple of years before new shrubberies were planted, an entrance opened via Park Avenue and a bandstand erected. [6]

Space between the park and Wrexham Road allowed the laying out of Park Road and the building of new houses there. This had scarcely started when the Queen died and the Edwardian Age began. One short terrace on the left hand side of an unnamed street –

A band playing in Jubilee Park on what might well have been the occasion of the Diamond Jubilee in 1897

which became Park Road -- is shown on the 1901 Ordnance Survey map of Whitchurch. By 1911 the street had been completed on both sides as part of a larger new housing development on both the north and south sides of Wrexham Road. This was laid out during the brief time that Edward VII was on the throne and was one of two significant suburban areas now developed. The other was the Salisbury Road and Victoria Road (later Queen's Road) area together with Station Road and Egerton Street, now Egerton Road, on the eastern edge of the town.

Above : *rear view of Park Road*

Endnotes

1. "Newetowne" was mentioned in a manor court record 1601 see H. B. Finch *Whitchurch in the reign of Queen Elizabeth* 1895 p21.
2. Shropshire Archives 212 Box 413 sketch plan of Mr Payne's pool [hereafter ShropA] Also *Salopian Journal* February 1829 and Whitchurch Rate Book 1827.
3. For more information see John Clayton *Whitchurch Hospitals and Medical Care* (2004) : 3rd Annual Report from Poor Law Commission to Parliament (1837 Accounts and Papers vol. xxxi p41-42)
4. *Whitchurch Herald* of 11 December 1869 [hereafter Herald
5. Herald reported these activities between February to May 1887
6. Herald 1897 March 27, April 3, June 26 : Whitchurch History and Archaeology Group Newsletter No. 64 January 1997 article by Joan Barton [hereafter WHAG]

❧ The Salisbury Road area : an Edwardian suburb ❧

Whitchurch got its railway station in 1858. This should have created a demand for an adequate roadway linking it to the main market and shopping centre. There isn't any evidence that improvement was immediate. In practice, the development of this side of town had to wait until Brownlow Street was constructed in the 1870s. Even then, there was no quick expansion of housing into the area. In the 1880s, a short row of cottages in Station Road, on the opposite side to the Police Station (1860), had stood since the seventeenth century and close by a rather dejected looking house, of indeterminate date, called itself the Railway Inn. Otherwise, the triangle of land bounded by Talbot Street, Station Road and the railway line on the east was open fields containing only a sand pit and one house adjacent to the station yard.

Talbot Street (previously Paradise Street) and Station Road (formerly Tin Hole Lane) did, however, attract builders in the 1890s to start constructing small rows of terraces and individual houses. They were probably mostly for rent and hardly counted as a planned development. As homes they were at a standard somewhat higher than the bulk of houses built before the 1870s. It may be that another stimulus to developing this area was the opening of Smith's Foundry, just beyond where Talbot Street petered out and Black Park Road began, alongside the railway to minimise transport costs.

Station Road and Talbot Street had been continuations of Green End. A gabled building in the angle formed at their

1911 Special Edition Ordnance Survey map

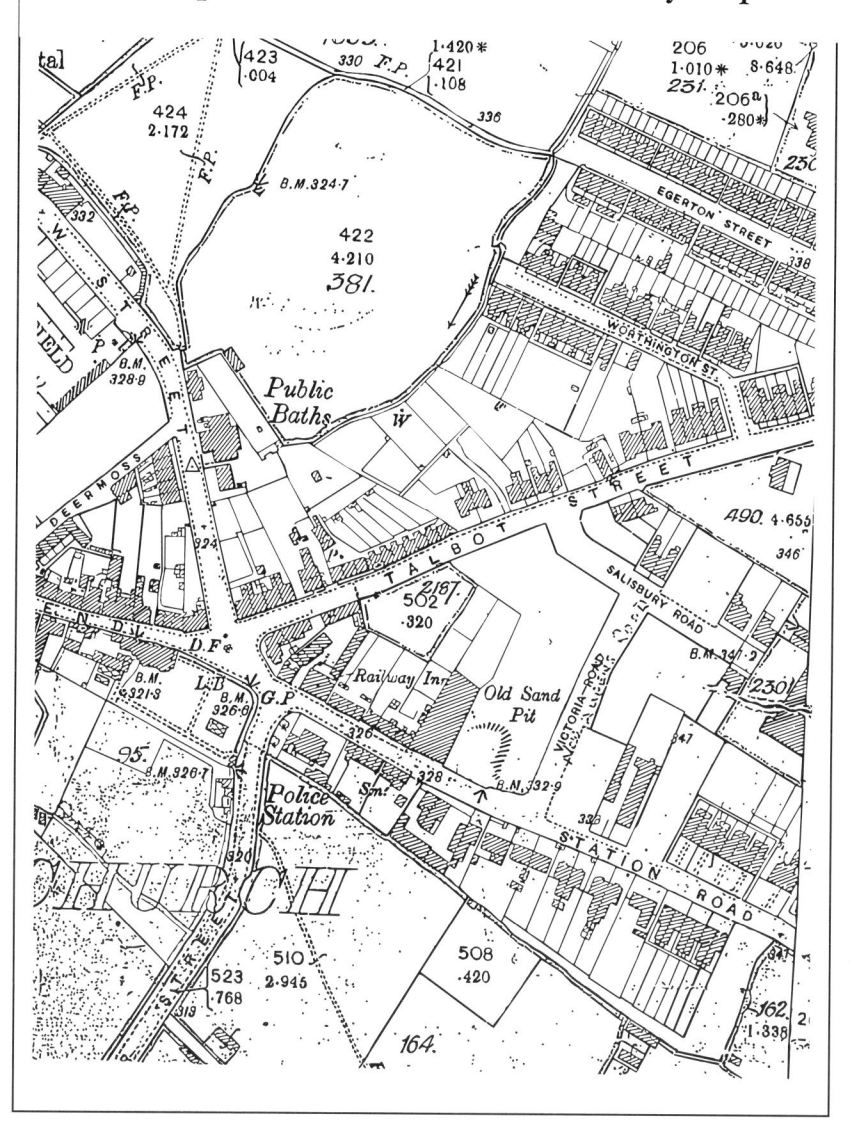

Right : *Seventeenth-century cottages in Station Road*

Below : *The two horses standing in Tin Hole Lane must have been photographed in the early 1870s before the construction of Brownlow Street*

Below right : *The Fountain on a postcard produced before 1900 was the centre piece of the junction of Green End and Brownlow Street. Solicitor's offices had replaced Henry Williams' premises*

Notice board reads
Henry Williams
Dealer in the best Lancashire, Ruabon Yard & Staffordshire Coals and Cannel. Bones, Salt etc
For Prices …
Coal Station   NB Agent for
Western Counties Manure Comp
Cannel was bituminous coal burning with a bright flame to make coal oil and gas
Photograph from T.C. Duggan *A History of Whitchurch* (1934)

The 14th Cheshire Regiment marched through Whitchurch from the station about 1914 on the way to Prees Heath Camp, passing Mulgrave Villas on their left

separation faced what had come to be open space with the laying out of Brownlow Street. This was graced by the erection of the Fountain which lent some elegance to the approach from the station to the principal town streets.

The north side of Station Road shows a wide variation in construction dates and a process of in-filling. Immediately beyond the Railway Inn and ancient timber-framed cottages a three-storey factory-looking structure was put up after 1902 which became Huxley's garage. Further towards the railway line, Richmond Terrace had been built by 1891. On the south side, a four-house terrace, Plain Field, was not built until 1899 and Mulgrave Villas was later in 1902.

Top right : *Plain Field in 2007*

Below right : *Mulgrave Villas in 2007*

Queen's Road (first known as Victoria Road) and Salisbury Road were marked out in the Edwardian period, but not immediately developed. One prime site was given to the new High School for Girls whose imposing façade closed off the end of Salisbury Road. Only three detached and a pair of semi-detached houses fronted the street before 1911, however. The houses on the corner of Queen's Road and Station Road, with their matching Flemish-looking gables, were not put up until after 1911. The width of the streets, back and front gardens, substantial projecting parlour windows with stone lintels and sills all betoken housing for the relatively prosperous middle classes.

Salisbury Road 2007

Semi-detached houses on corner of Station Road and Queen's Road

Talbot Street and a new street on its north side, Worthington Street, showed similar characteristics. The previous street name, Paradise Street, somewhat belied its character. Talbot Street thus had older terraced property at the town end, brick-built but without front garden space. In the 1890s houses of a quite different type were erected further along the street, spaced out, but semi-detached or in small blocks, with walled garden space at the front and bow windows. Distinctive decorative features were added attractions.

Talbot Street towards the town end in 2007

Egerton Road provides a nice contrast between properties built in the 1890s and those ten or fifteen years later. On the left hand side of the street adjoining terraces of brick cottages were the first to be erected. They are reminiscent of the older houses in Talbot Street, but have tiny front yards and appear to have rather more headroom as well as passage-ways giving access to the rear. Another recent photograph shows the other side of the street, built in the Edwardian not Victorian era, again with a garden yard separating the front door from the street but with bow windows adding distinction to the front parlour. Breaks in the rooflines identify separate blocks of development.

Talbot Street houses built in the 1890s

Contrasting terraces in Egerton Road in 2007 – those above were the first to be erected, and those to the right somewhat later and of the Edwardian age

West End and Chemistry

Late Victorian and Edwardian developments compared with 1839 Tithe Map

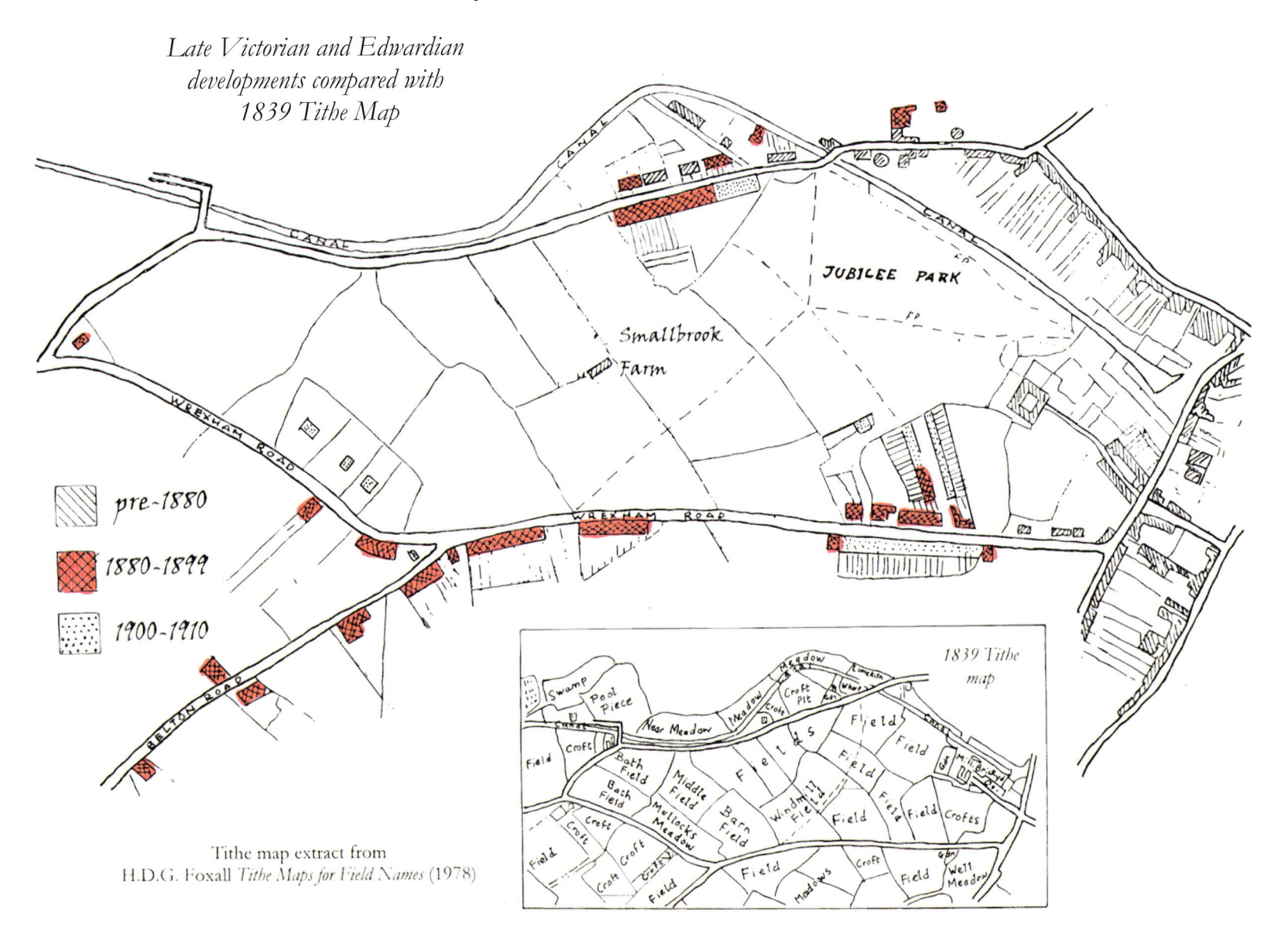

Legend:
- pre-1880
- 1880-1899
- 1900-1910

Tithe map extract from H.D.G. Foxall *Tithe Maps for Field Names* (1978)

1839 Tithe map

West End and Chemistry

One area of Whitchurch illustrating the slow rate of expansion since the late Victorian period is that bounded on the north by the Ellesmere canal and the road out to Chemistry and, on the south, by Wrexham Road. The north road is now Smallbrook Road with the stretch nearest the town earlier known as West End. They meet at Bathfields on the west, and on the east the boundary is defined by New Street.

Before 1880 one farmhouse stood more or less in the centre, Smallbrook Farm, and branching off New Street was an ancient row of timber-framed cottages called Scotland Street.[1] This led to a square building, remembered locally as a dairy house (marked as such on 1926 OS map). Close by, and tightly confined on the west bank of the canal, was an old corn mill, brickyard, malt kiln yard and stone yard. Otherwise this was agricultural land with no residential property at all.

Earlier surveyors, William Fowler and George Grey, did not leave any record of this district. Names of fields and their owners can be discovered from the 1839 tithe map and award. It is quite likely that the pattern of field boundaries and the multiplicity of owners and occupiers (nine owners, with twelve tenants, in addition to land kept in-hand by five of the owners) reflects the long-established status of this land as copyhold property in the manor of Whitchurch. It had been held traditionally by tradesmen and artisans residing in houses fronting the streets of the urban settlement. Among the owners and tenants in 1839 was a saddler in High Street, a linen and woollen merchant, a miller and corn dealer, and a boot and shoe maker in High Street.

Anne Hassall and William Churton stand out among landowners in this district. Hassall's property bordered the canal and included what amounted to a small industrial estate on New Street, on the opposite canal bank to the terminal wharf. This was close to the site of the old town mill. The 1827 Rate Book shows that Joseph Hassall owned a warehouse, wharf and nailor's shop in New Street, a house, garden, timber-yard and malt-kiln at Highgate, eleven houses with gardens in Havannah Buildings, and one house and garden in Scotland Street.

William Churton, in 1839, owned the fields on which Smallbrook Farmhouse stood. He leased the Windmill Field to Thomas Hall and kept the rest in hand. It is not as yet possible to say whether Hall occupied the house or not as it was built at the junction of the two halves of the estate. Churton was an auctioneer living in High Street, aged 60 with one son and three daughters at home according to the 1841 Census. His father, John, and he himself had been in business in the town, one way or another, for between them around 60 years.[2]

There was no change in the landscape or use of this area until late Victorian times, when the Jubilee Field was created at the end of the 1880s. Three small groups of dwellings were also put up around the same time – a terrace at West End on land which John Lowe had owned in 1839, a shorter terrace on Wrexham Road and another at an angle to it called Park Road on what had been one of Anne Hassall's fields, and, thirdly, a lone house called Bathfields on territory occupied by Thomas Jebb in 1839 and built some time after 1880 and before 1899. This was described as a detached house with stabling and garden in 1912. There were four bedrooms and two reception rooms and the house was equipped with a bath. It had apparently been bought in 1903 for £1,600 and almost immediately put up for sale again, unsuccessfully.[3]

Occupiers in the West End terrace in the mid-1890s were reputed to include Arthur Whittingham, who had a linen draper's shop in Watergate, Mrs Perkins, the widow of a well-known local cabinet maker, and Alfred Cooper, an auctioneer with an office in High Street.[4]

About the same time, and on the southern side of Wrexham Road further out from town, four more short terraces were built close to the lane leading off to Belton Farm. The sites for these seem to have been offered for sale in November 1887 to judge from an advertisement in the *Whitchurch Herald*.

Jubilee Park was a major change of use for land in this area, and further nibbling away at the edges continued in the Edwardian period. Park Road, for example, was completed on both sides before 1910 and Linden Avenue laid out where Thomas Cartwright's property of 1841 met the main road.

Park Road in 2007

SHROPSHIRE.

Freehold BUILDING SITES and Accommodation LANDS at WHITCHURCH, INN and LAND in TILSTOCK, and FARM in WHIXALL.

TO BE OFFERED FOR SALE BY AUCTION By COOPER AND SON

On THURSDAY, November 10th, 1887, in the ASSEMBLY ROOM, TOWN HALL, WHITCHURCH, at Two for Three o'clock punctually.

FREEHOLD BUILDING LAND, close to the town of Whitchurch and Railway Station, in the under-named Lots.

Lot 1.—Freehold Warehouse and Piece of Land, containing in the whole 3779 square yards or thereabouts, with a frontage to Green End Street of 140ft.

Lots 2, 3, 4, 5, 6, 7, 8, 9, 10, 11, 12, and 13, are Building Sites, as now staked out, each lot containing 1825 square yards or thereabouts, and a frontage of 70 feet to Station Road, leading from Green End Street to the Railway Station.

The whole of the above lots are in the occupation of Mr Henry Williams as yearly tenant.

BUILDING LAND, in Dodington, adjoining and near the Wrexham Road, about half a mile from Whitchurch, in the under-named Lots.

Lot 14.—Corner Building Site, as now staked out, containing 6184 square yards, with a frontage to the Wrexham Road of 290 feet, and the Belton Farm Road of 430 feet.

Lot 15.—Building Site, containing 3777 square yards, with a frontage to the Wrexham Road of 138ft.

Lot 16.—Building Site, containing 4039 square yards, with a frontage to Belton Farm Road of 142ft.

Lot 17.—Building Site, containing 3755 square yards, with a frontage to the said road of 142ft.

Lot 18—Building Site, containing 3281 square yards, with a frontage to the said road of 142ft.

Lots 14, 15, 16, 17, and 18, in the occupation of the representatives of the late John Green as yearly tenant.

LAND adjoining the Tarporley Road, half a mile from Whitchurch, in the under-named Lots

Lot 19.—Excellent Piece of Pasture Land and

Four sites for separate villa-type houses were also created just beyond the fork with Belton Lane. Three were named on an OS map dated 1911 as Sunnyside, Sandhurst and Glendee. A house was not marked on the latter nor apparently ever built. The fourth one was unidentified but the house was shown as built. This field was known as Mullock's meadow in 1839 and was the property of W.W.Brookes. Sunnyside and a small area of land just to the east belonged to I.J.Foulkes in 1910.

Finally, a short extension eastwards was made on the terrace at West End which continued to be a fashionable address among the town's businessmen.

In the 1920s and 1930s this district still did not attract much interest from house builders. It was 1937 before Meadow View Road was planned in a field which had been possessed by William Thomas in 1839. After the Second World War, however, a drastic change took place which is part of another stage in the development of Whitchurch.

One other, and an intriguingly named, district of Whitchurch, immediately west of Bathfields and Smallbrook Farm, is Chemistry. A farm with that name is found in the area, but it predates the acquisition of the name. This seems to refer to an oak-acid making business set up alongside the canal at the point where the main road swings south. According to THE FARMER'S ENCYCLOPAEDIA … EMBRACING ALL THE MOST RECENT DISCOVERIES IN AGRICULTURAL CHEMISTRY (1842) *"the bark of the oak is used for affording tannic acid in the manufacture of leather."* [5] Tanning was an art long practised in Whitchurch and shoe making had been a prominent trade in the town in the early nineteenth century.

The buildings which carried the identification 'The Chemistry' in a survey about 1912 were then a pair of cottages with small gardens attached. They were occupied by Samuel Woollam and owned by George Thomas Johnson. Across the narrow track leading to a bridge over the canal were a house and cow shed belonging to Joseph Hinde whose residence was in Birkenhead. Harry Hall lived there. [6]

The name Chemistry appears on the Ordnance Survey 1880 edition and in 1861 Thomas Jebb gave his address to the census enumerator as Wrexham Road Chemistry. Jebb was a farmer and miller, however, not an acid manufacturer. Moreover, he was a tenant and apart from his address there is no clue as to how his farm might have related to a chemical business. There is no reference in the Tithe Award for Whitchurch 1841 to either the address or an interest in chemistry in this district, which suggests that whatever chemical works was established it was somewhere between 1841 and 1861, and was so well-known that it had been adopted as a topographical location in the 1850s at the latest. Curiously, there is no mention of Chemistry in Bagshaw's *Directory 1851*, although Thomas Jebb is noted as a gentleman and a principal landowner living in Wrexham Road. On the other hand, T.C.Duggan once found an unspecified reference to an oak acid works near the town in 1824. [7]

Chemistry Farm is on the north side of the canal some score yards west of the bridge and immediately alongside the cut. The building dates back to 1805-10 and was then erected for the miller who had hitherto occupied what had once been called the New Mill on the Bridgewater estate. At the time this was William Jebb of the family who had been tenants of the Bridgewaters in New Mill Farm since at least 1778. The Tithe Award map 1839 clearly shows the site of the mill pool as 'swamp'. The mill had not completely ceased to operate although the miller's house had been demolished in 1805 – hence the new one by the canal and William Jebb's temporary home in a house owned by Joseph Hassall until his new one was finished. [8] William died in 1820 and his son Thomas took over and had the benefit of two 'new cast iron wheels, sockets, spindles and gudgeons for fixing and general repairs at the Mill and for iron pipes to convey water from the Mill pool upon the wheels' provided by the estate in 1831 at a cost of £330-0-0. [9] Clearly, this corn mill was thought to have a profitable future. In fact, it ceased to operate after 1861 and before 1880 when the site is noted on the Ordnance Survey map as an 'old corn mill'. The building had entirely disappeared when the 1901 map was prepared.

The farm presumably changed its name to Chemistry Farm after the association with corn milling ceased. It did not remain with the Jebbs, however. By 1912 it was occupied by Samuel Maddocks on a yearly tenancy from Earl Brownlow at an estimated annual rent of £60 for 24 acres and a house and farm buildings. [10]

The significant changes which had taken place in Chemistry by 1900 were the disappearance of both the oak acid business and the former New Mill, more recently renamed Old Mills. No interest had been shown in building anything else in the area before 1918 this being a traditionally agricultural district disturbed very little over many centuries except for the construction of the Ellesmere Canal in the 1790s.

Chemistry Farm in 2007

Endnotes

1. See National Monuments Records, Swindon, BF099763 Havannah Terrace 1-10 Scotland St. seven photos taken 9 Jan 1984
2. John Churton was parish clerk in 1803 collecting signatures of men volunteering for an infantry unit to defend Whitchurch against Napoleon.
3. Land Tax Valuation Survey (1910) at The National Archives IR58/76084, property number 1507 [hereafter Land Tax Survey]
4. Information from Mary Perry 2006.
5. The author was Cuthbert W. Johnson.
6. Land Tax Survey IR58/76078, number 943; IR58/76084 number 1518
7. T.C.Duggan *A History of Whitchurch* (1935 p51)
8. Information from Lindsay Green see ShropA 212/611/Bundle Bridgewater Estate Disbursement Accounts
9. See Shrop R&R 212/611/241. Thomas Jebb in Bagshaw's 1851 Directory was not only listed as a gentleman but also as a miller at 'Old Mills'.
10. Land Tax Survey IR58/76084, number 1528

This drinking fountain which once stood in the centre of the road junction where Green End met Brownlow Street was the gift of John Churton in 1882 in memory of his wife Ann. Its slender form, ornate gothic tracery and inset bas-relief panels reflect the architectural taste of the mid-Victorian period. Whitchurch had few other street decorations to match it. The façade of the Town Hall and Market 1872 was something of a precedent.

The postcard view of about 1900 shows that the provision of free fresh water was complemented by two gas lamps to illuminate an important street crossing. Churton's offices can be seen immediately facing the fountain.

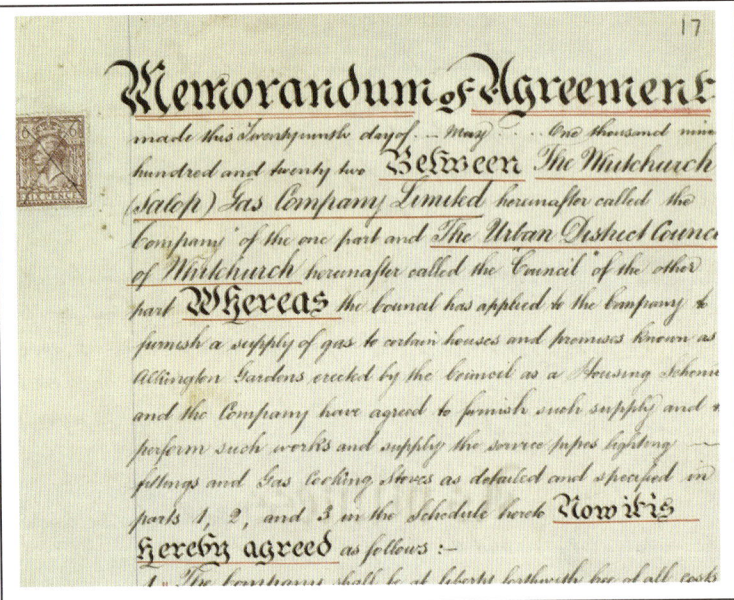

Alkington Gardens in 2007 and evidence of gas supplies in 1922

Local Authority housing

One obviously new feature of the expansion of Whitchurch after 1918 was a series of housing estates built by the Urban District Council. All local government authorities were obliged from 1919 to survey the housing needs of their populations. These had to be met by planned developments under council control. The result was estates of what were popularly called council houses, built in a variety of types, but only for rent, sometimes covering large areas of former agricultural land. They were a significant contribution to raising living standards for sections of the population never before enjoying even modest comfort and convenience at home.

The national legislation which initiated this action was part of the move to peace at the end of the Great War. It aimed at meeting immediate needs, not creating a revolution in housing the working classes. In practice, insufficient numbers and inefficient distribution of houses over the country as a whole ensured that local authorities became permanently involved in building and maintaining an ever-increasing stock of houses. It took another war to bring about the social revolution, but the process began in 1919. In the 1980s, a Conservative government abruptly put an end to the whole project.

The earliest houses erected by Whitchurch UDC were in Alkington Gardens in 1922. This was a small scheme of neatly laid out semi-detached houses, just beyond what was Dodington Brewery, where Kingsway (then called Gig Lane) joins Alkington Road.

Planning started in 1920 but it is not well documented in the archives available today.[1] Virtually the only thing which can be recorded with confidence is that gas was piped in for light and cooking, a step-change in facilities for the working families who moved into these homes.[2]

Newspaper reports at the time of local authority meetings reflected a variety of attitudes on the extent to which the town had a housing problem. On the one hand, the editor of the *Whitchurch Herald* at one time was all in favour of collecting whatever benefits national government could confer, yet at other times poured cold water on proposed actions. Some councillors, on the other hand, considered the town much in need of new, improved homes for working people and favoured ambitious plans.

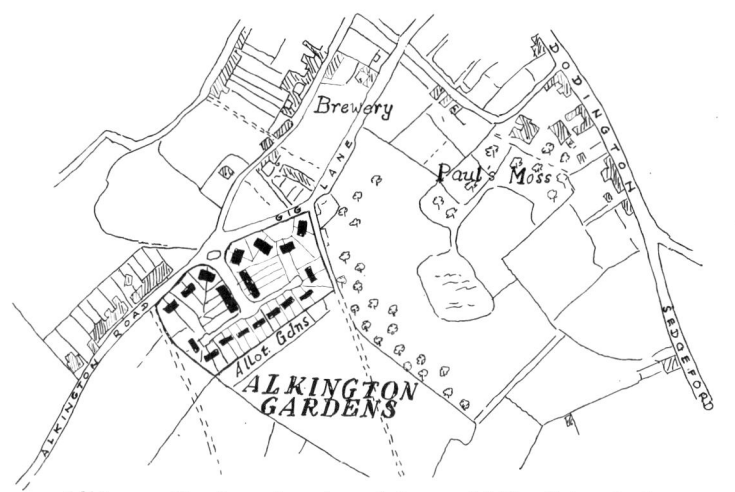

Alkington Gardens site adapted from a 1930 edition Ordnance Survey map

One memory of childhood partly spent in Alkington Gardens was of a two-bedroom house which had a single living-room on the ground floor with windows front and back. The view at the rear was over open land popularly called 'Soldiering Fields'. There was a kitchen with a small black range for cooking and, more particularly, for heating water – "a luxury as it had not been available in my birthplace, my grandparent's house in Alkington Road, built in the 1890s and with only one cold water tap in the kitchen". Gas lighting is remembered, but there is some uncertainty about a gas cooker. Grandparents undoubtedly cooked on an open fire and in an oven to one side. 'But the biggest luxuries of all were the bathroom and indoor lavatory, both on the ground floor.' [3]

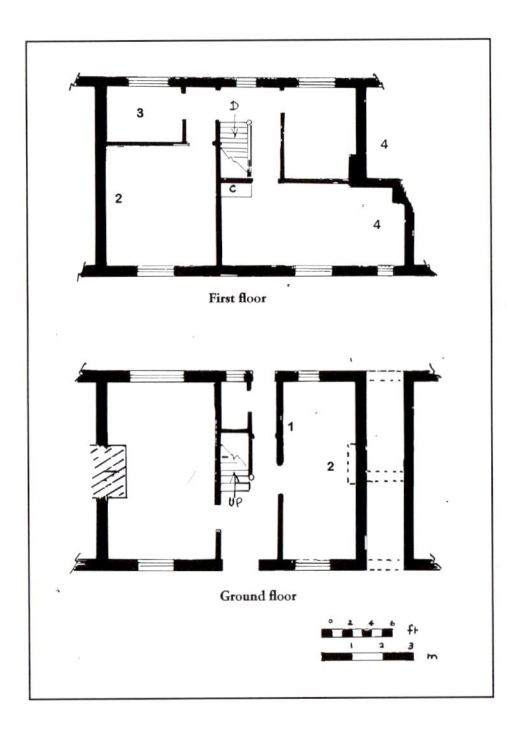

A second scheme became necessary in 1928. This was a three-part plan for houses at sites along Wrexham Road, secondly in Rosemary Lane and also, on the opposite side of the town, off Station Road. George Edge and Son and A.Davies, of Castle Hill, had the contract and the same type of house was put up on Wrexham Road and in Rosemary Lane. The front door opened into a twelve-foot square living room, and a scullery with a bathroom to one side was at the rear. Access to a lavatory was from an outside door immediately alongside the back door out of the scullery. Stairs to bedrooms led out of the living room. A gas cooker was placed in the scullery. Altogether ninety-four houses were in the scheme. [4]

Alkington Gardens : terrace properties as found in February 2008

1. Kitchen, probably originally divided with a bathroom in rear section

2. Kitchen chimney breast has been removed

3. Upstairs bathroom made by dividing principal bedroom

4. Front bedroom stretches over passage way at front of house. This way of extending a bedroom is followed in the adjoining house using space over passage at the rear.

Rosemary Lane in 2007

The editor of the *Whitchurch Herald* kept a close eye on the housing policies of the Urban District Council from February 1919 when the issue first arose. Early suspicions of the need for subsidised houses, when ratepayers had to meet part of the costs, evaporated somewhat after Alkington Gardens became occupied. On 7 July 1923 it was reported in the newspaper that

'... the Council spent a considerable amount of time on Tuesday evening in deciding between the rival claims for a vacant house, it looks as though we have a long way to go before the normal needs of the district are likely to be satisfied. Here we have two ex-servicemen, both showing good credentials, both in absolute need of housing accommodation, and the two so difficult to decide between that the successful applicant eventually won the prize by a majority of one! It is lamentable. And we are quite sure that the Counsellors themselves, and the great bulk of their constituents, are fully alive to this, and are desirous that no unnecessary time shall be lost in the easement of the situation which is discreditable from a national point of view and unsatisfactory in its local and personal aspects. Incidentally, it may not be out of place to say that the Council have especial reason for satisfaction as to the appearance of 'Alkington Gardens'. The tenants have developed their resources in the most praiseworthy way, with the result that the appearance of the whole "estate" is creditable and gratifying in the extreme. What should we have done, after all, without these forty houses?'

Whitchurch Herald 23 August 1919

Almost immediately after this development another was started in Talbot Street, in 1929, later called Talbot Crescent. For this the builder was Alun Edwards from Wrexham. He worked to plans for three types of house, one of which was semi-detached with a parlour and bow window at the front and a thirteen-foot square kitchen behind. A tiny scullery opened off the kitchen and from this there was access to a coal store. The front door opened into a hallway out of which there were stairs to an upper floor. An important advance in design was built-in storage space, and, perhaps even more significant, a narrow yard edged by a brick wall separated the front door from the street pavement. [5]

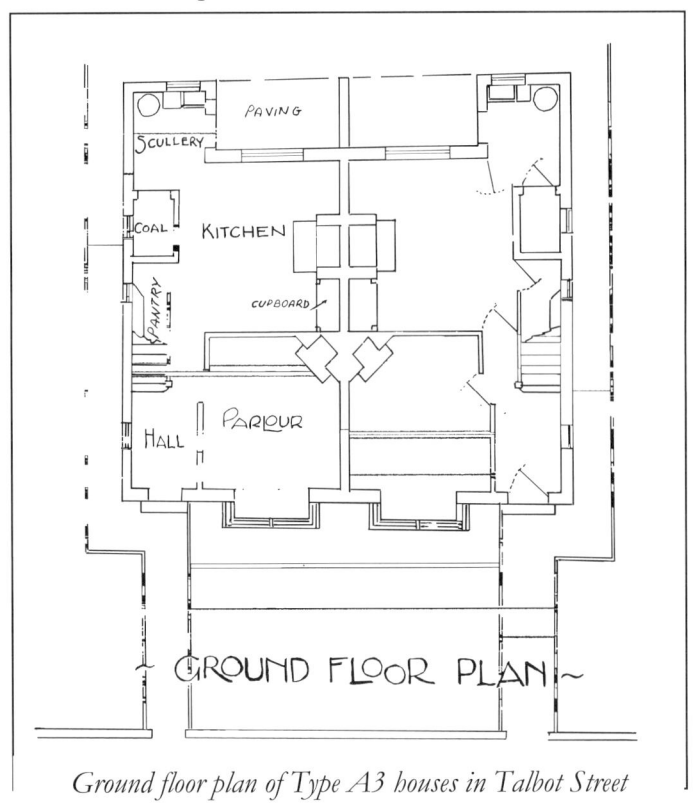

Ground floor plan of Type A3 houses in Talbot Street

In 1936 what was called Scheme Number 6 was planned for Egerton Road. This was a mixture of semi-detached houses and terraces in what was later called George Street. They were all of the non-parlour type and had either three or four bedrooms. The builder was George Edge & Son and A. Davies. Thirty-five cottages were planned and the total cost to Whitchurch UDC was £10,745. [6] It was intended that all would be complete by the end of January 1937. Among the surviving records there are a number of plans which suggest that some considerable amendments were required to the original designs which had been provided by the architect and surveyor to the Urban District Council, M.W.Sowden.

More could be said about the reasons why Whitchurch needed council houses in the twenty years following the end of the First World War. A large increase in population was probably not among them, whereas changes in social attitudes and aspirations were. These were homes of a distinctly improved character as against some of the stock of housing bequeathed by mid-Victorian speculators. They were for rent, but then this was still a period when working people expected to live in rented accommodation all their lives. Certainly the better off, with steady jobs during a time of economic depression, were aiming to own their own homes in larger numbers and building societies expanded to provide the mortgages. Local authority housing schemes were obviously necessary to Whitchurch, however, and they may well have been an opportunity for families to move out of overcrowded parental homes.

From 1930 onwards a succession of acts of Parliament laid obligations on local authorities to demolish unsanitary properties incapable of improvement. A Housing Act in 1935 required that a survey be made of the extent of overcrowding as a specific cause of acute social problems.

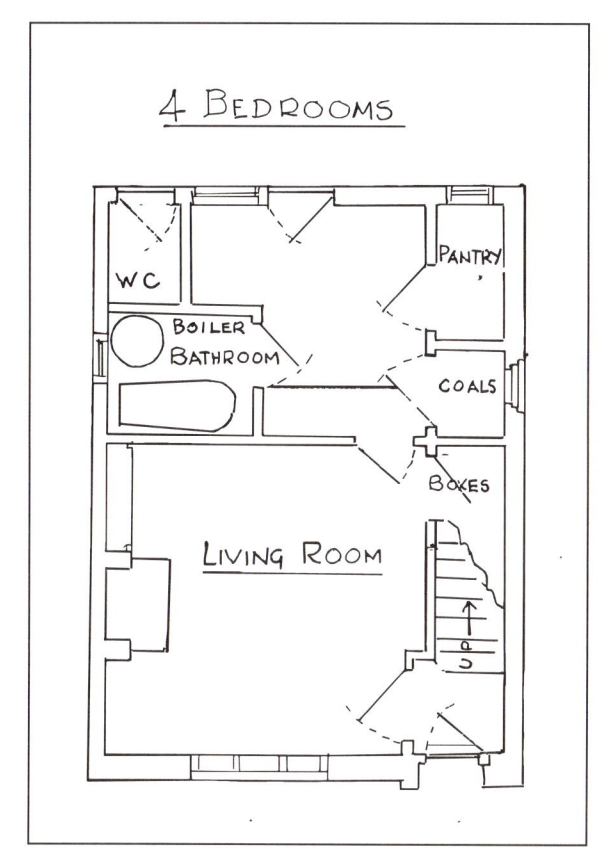

Left above : *Ground plan for a four bedroom house in the Egerton Road scheme in 1936*

Right above : *Wayland Road was a late 1930s development for the Urban District Council*

Right below : *Houses in the 1928 scheme with a local builder as contractor*

Whitchurch officials duly carried out an inquiry so as to identify areas for slum clearance.[7] These were scattered about the central district of the town in yards and alleys, behind properties fronting main streets as well as in Newtown, Yardington and Castle Hill. For example, properties in Liverpool Road where thirty-three people lived in seven rented dwellings were listed, and demolished in 1938 despite protests from the owners. Eight unoccupied houses in Barlow's Yard – on the west side of High Street immediately opposite Church Street - and others with fifteen inhabitants in them were taken down in 1937. Raven's Yard, behind Watergate, and Shard's Yard were also listed and 38 people had to be re-housed. In total, at this stage, 124 adults and children were moved out of ancient timbered cottages to new council houses.

Above : *E.J.Phipson's watercolour in the 1890s of Barlow's Yard in an earlier period*
Below : *Newtown properties in the course of demolition in 1970*

The consequences of a second World War exacerbated housing difficulties. In addition to the backlog of clearances from pre-war days there was a shortage of new houses as none had been built since 1940, and there were rising expectations about living conditions built up while the nation put everything into a war effort. Whitchurch had recourse to the emergency measure of erecting prefabricated homes although hardly on the scale seen in the likes of Coventry or Liverpool. They were put up as required by the Housing Act 1944. One site used was in the grounds of the former Workhouse and another, called Sedgeford, on land bought from J. Minshall, F.Williams and E.M.L.Thompson. As soon as possible this became the place for permanent housing and the site was extended with land bought from Mrs. F.W.Simon of Sedgeford House.[8] Out of these moves grew what is popularly referred to as the Queensway estate.

The corollary of erecting more new council houses was removal of the remaining condemned properties in yards off High Street and Yardington, cottages in Station Road and Scotland Road, and the whole of Newtown. This was a process still going on in the 1970s. Timbered buildings, some three hundred years or so old, were typically tiny, lacking light, air and water, and most often inhabited by the elderly poor. They were scattered among houses of later date and sounder construction. Old Mr Tapley in the row in Station Road, just beyond the Railway Inn, is remembered by one of the former school-girls who had to pass his door every day. These cottages soon flooded in heavy rain. In a neighbouring yard a clogmaker can be recalled who carved toys to increase his trade. Off Yardington were other ancient properties which had been condemned by council officers, but sometimes thought by councillors to be capable of renovation. Certainly one memory of them is that they proved surprisingly difficult to tear down. Mr. F.Saunders, the Urban District Council surveyor, plays an important role in memories of this feature of Whitchurch's post-second world war social history.[9]

At least two other major estates were laid out with local authority housing. The smaller one was an extension to the pre-war development off Egerton Road called Elizabeth Street. This was initiated in 1946 with Whitchurch (Salop) Contractors Ltd doing the work. Three types of houses were shown on the plans. It was a most unfortunate time to be building homes as shortages of materials, especially timber and steel, forced prices up and the contractors frequently found it necessary to seek additional funding from the local authority.[10]

The other much larger project was on the fields of the former Smallbrook Farm between Wrexham Road and Smallbrook Road. Three people owned the land prior to the Urban District Council acquiring it and negotiations seem to have started in 1951. By September 1953 the first stages were in hand with 64 houses in Thompson Drive and Sharps Drive. The latter appears to have been named after one of the former landowners.

A recent view of the site of the former Smallbrook Farm

One summary of this post-war expansion of Whitchurch, and the role of the local authority supervising it, was published in a Town Guide about 1968.
The Urban Council have been very much alive to the expanding housing needs. In addition to the 20 Temporary Houses in Sedgeford, 80 permanent type were built on Egerton Road Site of 3 and 4 bedroom type. A further 133 were built on the Sedgeford site, 188 on Smallbrook site and 4 Flats in Claypit Street. Recently a further 2 on Bath Street, 8 more Flats in Claypit Street, 8 more Flats on Sedgeford and now a further 44 units on Smallbrook. The

latter includes 2,3 and 4 bedroom types, a type larger than normal type with bay windows; also 8 one bedroom Flats. This Estate has now been completed, bringing the total number of houses built by the U.D.C. to over 700.

A large scheme of re-development is at present being prepared for the Newtown- Yardington clearance area.' [11]

In practice, Newtown was not completely cleared until after 1970. Its disappearance marked an important stage in the story of the townscape of Whitchurch just as its creation in Tudor times had signalled physical growth and increased economic activity.

In the last quarter of the twentieth century Whitchurch once more owed its development more to commercial interests than local authority responsibilities. It also lost its administrative independence in 1974 which was another major marker in the town's history.

One of the mayors a few years after local government reorganisation summed up this last stage as one giving the town a new face as *'we have seen the post-war estates grow up and mature into the Elizabeth Street-Bath Street areas, the Queensway estate, the Sharps Drive, Thompson Drive and Caldecott Crescent area.'*

He noted that *'medieval Newtown has ceased to exist, being replaced by Castle Court Flats, and other buildings. In the High Street we have seen the construction of the new Civic Centre, while the White Lion Meadow, the scene of bygone football battles, carnivals and other local events now forms part of the Car Park, the complex of buildings of the new Swimming Bath, the Fire Station, the Youth Centre and sites for future developments.'* [12]

Smallbrook Farm estate in 2007

End notes

1. ShropA DA15/15/25 Contract dated 20 May 1920 for Walter Webb as architect to design first housing scheme for Whitchurch UDC. This chapter is based upon documents found in the Whitchurch Urban District Council collection in Shropshire Archives under reference number DA15. Hereafter only the number for each document is given.
2. DA15/743/17.
3. Information from a private source.
4. DA15/725/1
5. DA15/743/22-27
6. DA15/725/3
7. DA15/606/1
8. DA15/135/8-23
9. Private information
10. DA15/135/17/7
11. *Whitchurch Town Guide* c 1968 p25 with note also on private house building
12. R.F.C. Hughes in *Whitchurch Town Guide* (no date c1980)

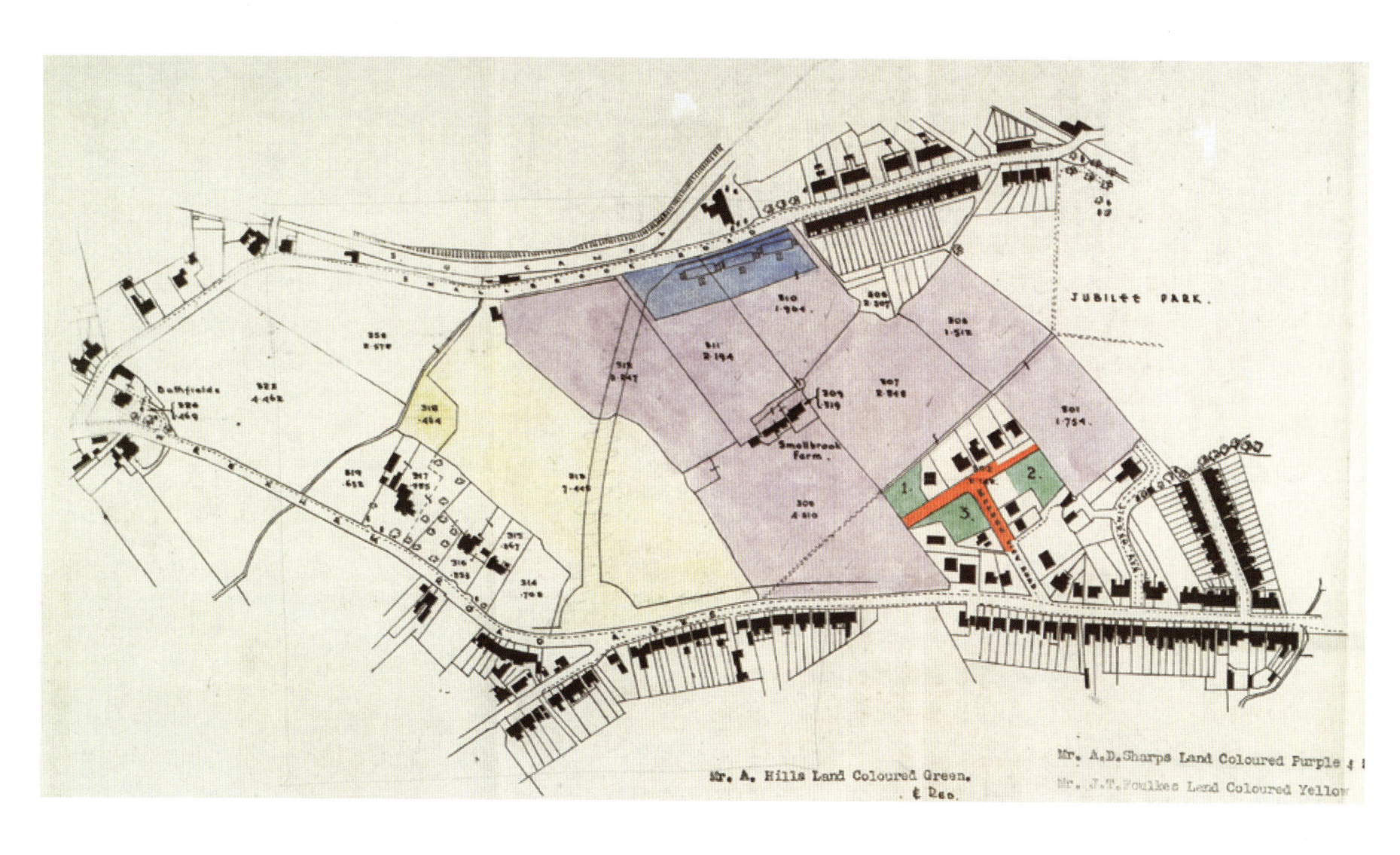

1952 Plan of the lands around Smallbrook Farm purchased by the Urban District

The growth of Whitchurch 1761 - 1970

The map on the opposite page has been specially drawn by Jean North to illustrate the pattern of developments since George Grey produced his plan of Whitchurch town in 1761. The dates which mark changes have been determined by the availability of original maps, not because of some other significance. It isn't possible at this scale to show every detail, street by street, but a general outline of expansion beyond the central core is displayed. The darkest colours indicate the oldest districts and blank areas were not built on before 1970. More recently, of course, there has been a lot of building, especially the bus station and adjacent supermarkets in the area of the former town pool and White Lion meadows

Two features stand out. One is the way that, over time, Whitchurch has changed from being a linear town roughly north-south in alignment, to being more east-west in form. The pattern of major streets has not significantly altered with the obvious exception that a by-pass now takes traffic on a route well to the west of the built-up area. This is the second of the map's main features, but one which also highlights the continued importance of road transport in the twentieth century. In the period illustrated by the map a canal was dug and then filled in, and railways have come and almost gone. There still is a station on the Crewe to Hereford and Cardiff line, but the cross-country Cambrian Railway track has been removed. Roads, by contrast, are fixed points in the urban landscape.

It is also clear on the map that perhaps the most rapid expansion of housing took place in the 1950s and 1960s. This was the age of planned development by the Urban District Council. For whatever reason, new estates were scattered around the town leaving open spaces in between, thus preserving something of the paradoxically rural aspect of the town, traditionally an important element in its character. Maps cannot directly illuminate every facet of a community and its life, but the more the ground is covered by concrete and tarmac the less likely it is that those living in the place will feel in touch with the countryside. A map of Whitchurch in 2008 will almost certainly show a contraction in open space. Jubilee Park, as a consequence, will stand out as an even more valuable green lung in the late Elizabethan age than it was said to be when Victoria's long reign was celebrated by its opening.

Overall, the impression of Whitchurch created by seeing this timed sequence of change is that of a patchwork of development. Given the slow rate of population growth, relative to that nationally, this is hardly surprising. A map of land use at one specific date could be set alongside this summary of change over time. This would throw into relief other important facets of the town's history, especially if it differentiated between retail shops and offices of professionals as against manufacturing businesses, local authority properties, domestic housing, and services such as hotels, petrol stations and car show rooms. Perhaps some day this will be done!

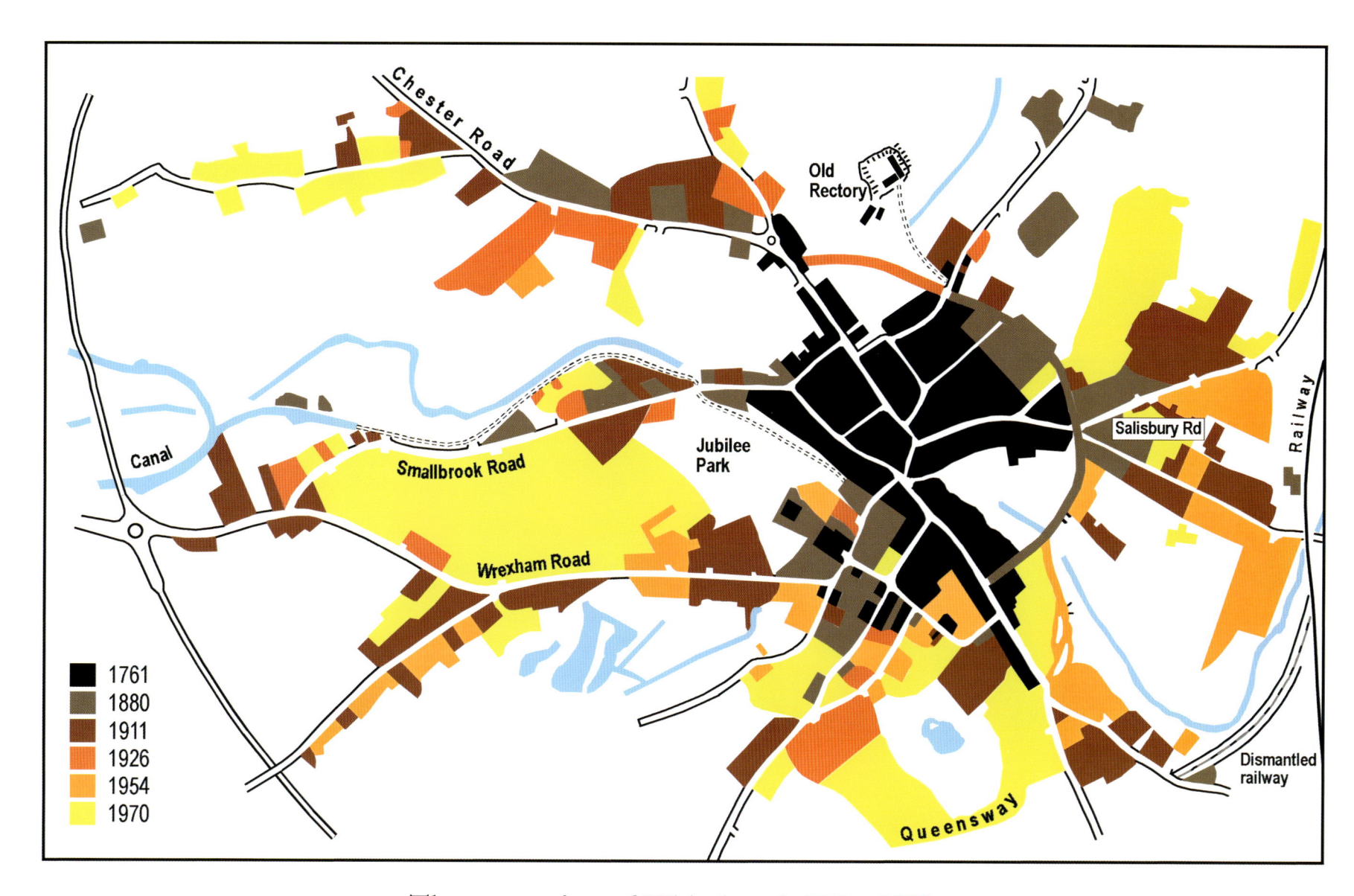

The expansion of Whitchurch 1761 - 1970

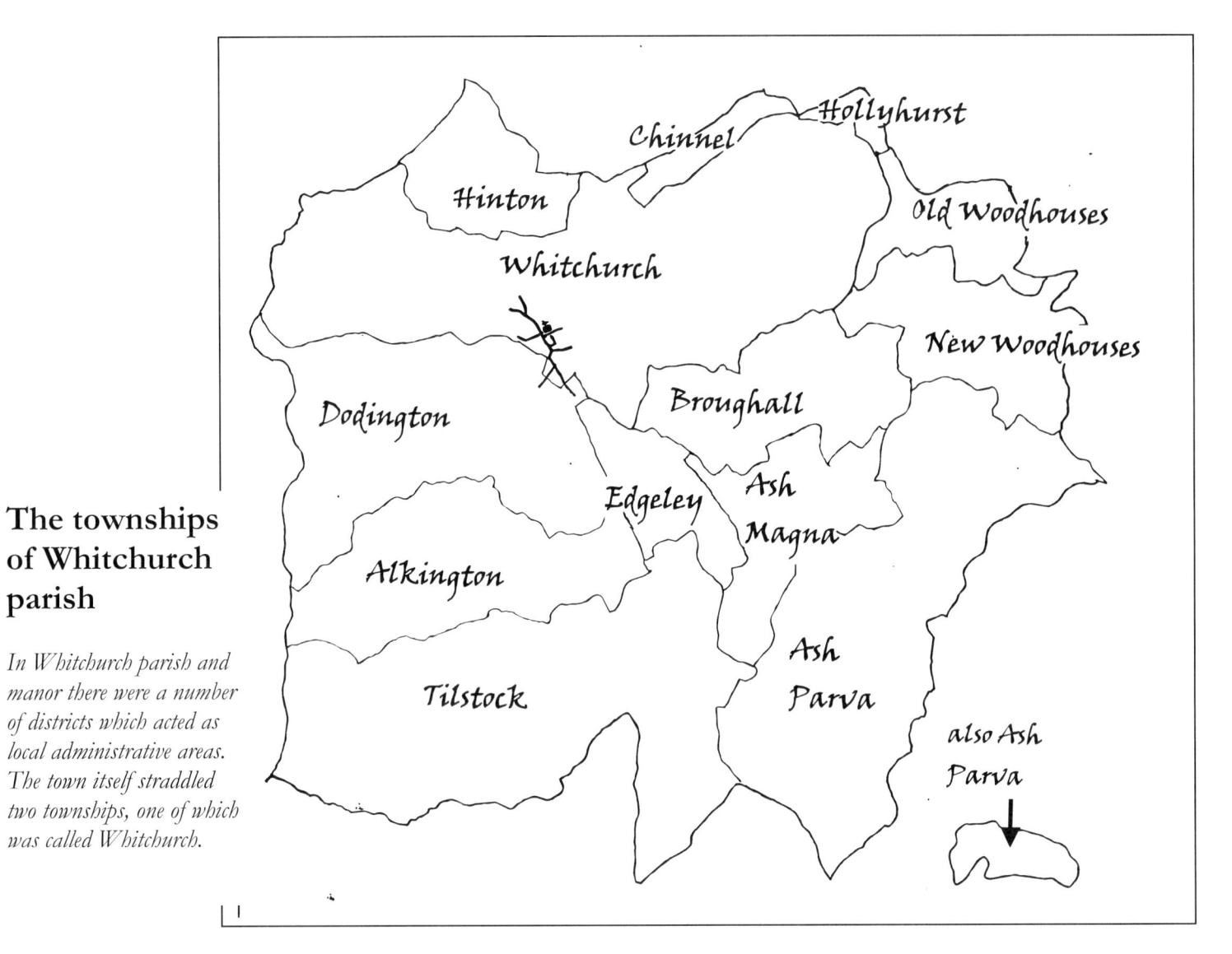

The townships of Whitchurch parish

In Whitchurch parish and manor there were a number of districts which acted as local administrative areas. The town itself straddled two townships, one of which was called Whitchurch.

The history of the town cannot easily be separated from that of the two authorities which acted as governing bodies over this whole area. Originally, the manor with its courts was the principal agent of administration, but by the eighteenth century a parish Vestry meeting was becoming more important in community business.

William Fowler and seventeenth-century maps

There's a lot to learn from maps about how the urban settlement in Whitchurch expanded after 1761. The earliest maps we have, however, are of parts of the much larger rural district to which the name applied – that is of the parish and manor of Whitchurch. Among them is an intriguing pair by William Fowler, drawn in 1651, showing parts of the countryside around the town. They open a wider window into the past with views of the estates of the Egerton family, earls and then dukes of Bridgewater.

This family acquired the manors of Whitchurch and Dodington in 1598 when Sir Thomas Egerton, father of the first Earl of Bridgewater, bought them from the Earl of Shrewsbury's brother, Edward. This was, in practice, the parish served by St. Alkmund's church containing ten townships whose names are still familiar as districts of North Shropshire. Collectively, they were called Whitchurch after the township containing the High Street settlement, and Dodington township gave its name to the street. Of the other townships, the only one which might have become an urban settlement was Tilstock, but it never gathered a population much larger than any of the others : two Ashes, (Magna and Parva), two Woodhouses (Old and New), Edgeley, Alkington, and the combined Hollyhurst and Chinnell.

The earls of Bridgewater amassed several large properties in Lancashire, Cheshire, Shropshire and Buckinghamshire. Their chief estate was at Ashridge in Hertfordshire.

Whitchurch manor was not a particularly profitable possession but from time to time Bridgewater's agents submitted accounts which listed tenants and the rents they owed. These papers provide numerous clues to the Whitchurch story.[1] In addition, twice in the early seventeenth century, the manorial properties were mapped – tantalisingly so to the modern researcher for a sufficient number of the plans exist to suggest that two surveyors, at different times, plotted the whole area, but in neither case has a complete set of their drawings survived. The only additions to the list are two anonymous sketches, undated and quite different in style. One was of *'Tilstocke Park'* and the other of a stream which ran across the main highway, appropriately called Watergate at this point, flowing down to power the town mill. This latter is probably the oldest of the maps at the disposal of the historical explorer. It is examined later in a section devoted to Whitchurch mills.

William Fowler, surveyor

The one identifiable surveyor was William Fowler. He clearly put his name, and the date 1651, on a map of the 'Bubney Forest' section of Whitchurch township. This is copied here exactly as he drew it. His other plan was of part of Dodington, presumably done at the same time. It's shown here in an edited form to emphasise individual farm boundaries, to display the names of their occupants and to locate their dwellings. The original map gave this information in a separate schedule (see pages 47 and 48).

William Fowler's signature on his map of Bubney

William Fowler was almost certainly the brother of Thomas Fowler the rector of Whitchurch, and both owed their appointments to the first Earl of Bridgewater. Thomas became rector in 1631 and William was doing survey work in the manor measuring property by the end of 1641 at the latest. [2] The 1651 maps were produced for the second Earl of Bridgewater who inherited the estate at the end of 1649. Fowler was evidently a mapmaker of some skill though there is no evidence as to how he acquired his knowledge or practised his art before 1651. Several of his surveys of other parts of the Bridgewater estates, as well as drawings he produced for Sir Richard Leveson, for example, are witness to his capabilities, and at least eleven items of his work are stored in various public archives today. All were made after the plans of Bubney and Dodington were completed.

The Fowler brothers were of a family based at Pendeford in Staffordshire, and two of the several sons of Walter Fowler. [3] He had extensive properties in the parish of Tettenhall and was closely related to at least three other families of Fowlers, all descendents of Sir William Fowler and his wife Cecily. The probate record of William's possessions at death in 1664 included an inventory and as this was made jointly by Walter Fowler junior and Daniel Rowley the assumption is made that he was Walter's brother. One of the three items valued was 'Bookes & Instruments belonging to survey - £5.' All told, his assets were only worth £35. He was noted as of Pendeford in the parish of Tettenhall – all of which links William the mapmaker to the Fowlers of Pendeford. [4]

William may have been born around 1610 as the seventh child of his father Walter and mother Margaret. [5] At some point he married Sarah Burton, daughter of Edward Burton of Longnor in Shropshire, and they had at least three children. Two were boys baptised in 1643 (Robert) and 1645 (William) respectively, [6] and his daughter, Alice, was named in the probate documents. As she was to administer his estate with Daniel Rowley the boys must have failed to reach manhood. Sarah died in October 1653 and William on 8 September 1664. [7]

As brother to Thomas, the rector of Whitchurch, William Fowler had access to the Bridgewater estate and the evidence that he acted as a surveyor for the first Earl

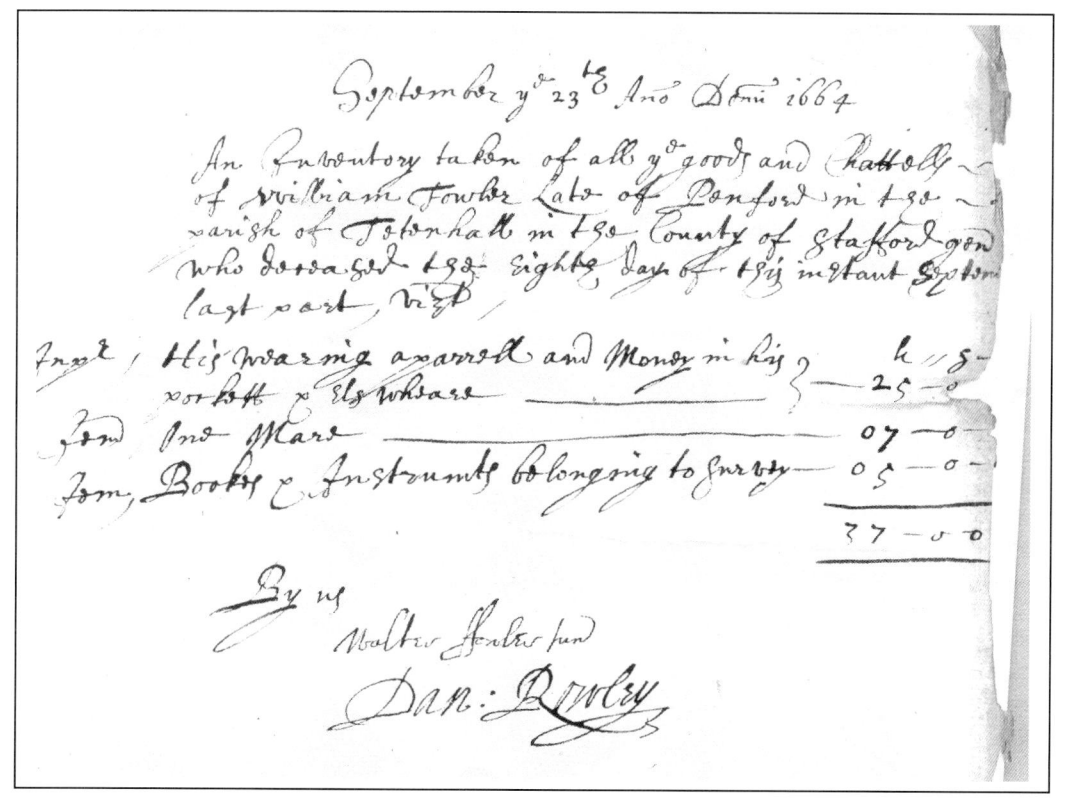

Inventory of the possessions of William Fowler at his death in 1664

before the winter of 1642 is the mention of his name in the roll of tenants-at-will compiled by Richard Hyde and John Aldersey in February that year. This was in connection with the measurement of a piece of ground over which there may have been some dispute.[8] Not long after that his career was bound up with larger conflicts of a civil war and challenges to the established authorities of monarchy and church. What happened to William is not known, but Thomas was driven out of his parish by the Parliamentary troops of Sir William Brereton in 1643. He subsequently refused to submit to the victorious Puritan authorities, for example not signing the Solemn League and Covenant. In April 1649 his estate was sequestered, and he compounded for its return at a cost of £130 for his delinquency 'in going into Shrewsbury when a garrison for the King.'[9]

It isn't possible to explain why there are only two parts of the manor of Whitchurch on maps by Fowler. The best guess is that he was commissioned to plot only certain types of tenancies in any case, and plans for other townships have simply been lost. From the Bubney and Dodington sheets it would appear that he was not asked to survey copyhold land, and this impression is reinforced by the other set of plans, ascribed to a mystery surveyor, which were clearly drawn on this same basis. If this was the case, the maps plot holdings let out on a lease of some kind – either by indenture for a specific term, or 'at will'. From the earl's point of view these properties would have been the most valuable on his estate because there was an opportunity to increase rents from time to time. This was not possible on land held by right of copyhold, the rents being fixed by ancient custom of the manor.

The reason why William Fowler was commanded to make his survey in 1651 is another of the mysteries associated with these maps. It is not certain whether they were produced to clarify the Earl's ownership rights, or to assess the value of his property for Commissioners responsible to Parliament. They were collecting fines levied on the territories of supporters of Charles I in the civil wars It is most likely that the second Earl of Bridgewater felt an urgent need to assess the value of his assets and to record the size and exact location of his estates. Curiously though, his inquiries appear to have been confined to Whitchurch manor. He had inherited all his lands from his father in 1649 when he was about twenty-seven years old. Both he and his father initially supported the king in the civil wars which flared up in 1642, but came to occupy an equivocal position as a Commonwealth government evolved to replace a monarchical one. The first Earl has been said to be lucky that Charles I dismissed him from his post as Lord President of the Council of the Welsh Marches for refusing more contributions to the royal fighting fund [10] He did not willingly subscribe to signing declarations in favour of Parliament either, but he died eleven months after the king without attracting too much enmity from the Rump Parliament then in control of the state. There were threats, nevertheless, of sequestration hanging over the king's aristocratic allies, many of whom lost their estates as a penalty for their 'delinquency'. The second Earl was doubly in jeopardy because he took over lands burdened with enormous debts. These were the consequence of bad investment decisions taken by his father who had helped to finance a son-in-law's trading ventures which were profitless. [11] In April 1651 the earl was arrested and examined by the authorities as to his supposed involvement in royalist affairs. Bail was allowed on his own surety of £10,000 and that from two others of £5,000 each. It is hardly to be wondered why he needed to have his financial resources assessed. He promised not to do anything 'prejudicial to the present government', and he was careful to stay away from London. [12] He sought to escape further financial problems by taking no part in public life. Instead, he worked to improve his Ashridge house and park which, far from relieving himself of debt, added considerably to it. [13] It would be natural in these circumstances for the young Earl to employ a mapmaker to describe the extent of an estate hitherto mapped in a colourful, but rather crude fashion at a date not now known and by a surveyor whose name has been lost. [14]

❧ Fowler's maps ☙

Fowler's map of Bubney shows a field pattern which corresponds closely with that observed, and mapped again, long afterwards. The individual holdings can be identified by a key allocating a different letter to each tenant and a number to each field. On the same sheet is a schedule giving the size of fields and their names. Rents due and conditions of leases may have been recorded, but if so this was done separately and the papers have disappeared. Even without the accompanying documentation the map vividly demonstrates the concentrated form of each farm and the location of the various farmsteads in this one section of Whitchurch township. Twelve men are recorded as leaseholders, and though it is not certain that they actually lived in the farmsteads it is likely that they did. Between them they held 388 acres. It is very noticeable that Fowler marked the boundaries of holdings where these were in common with copyholders' land also in Whitchurch township, but not elsewhere. Two manors to the north and west and the township of Dodington in the south were named as adjacent, but no individuals with neighbouring lands were stated.

Bubney Forest 1651

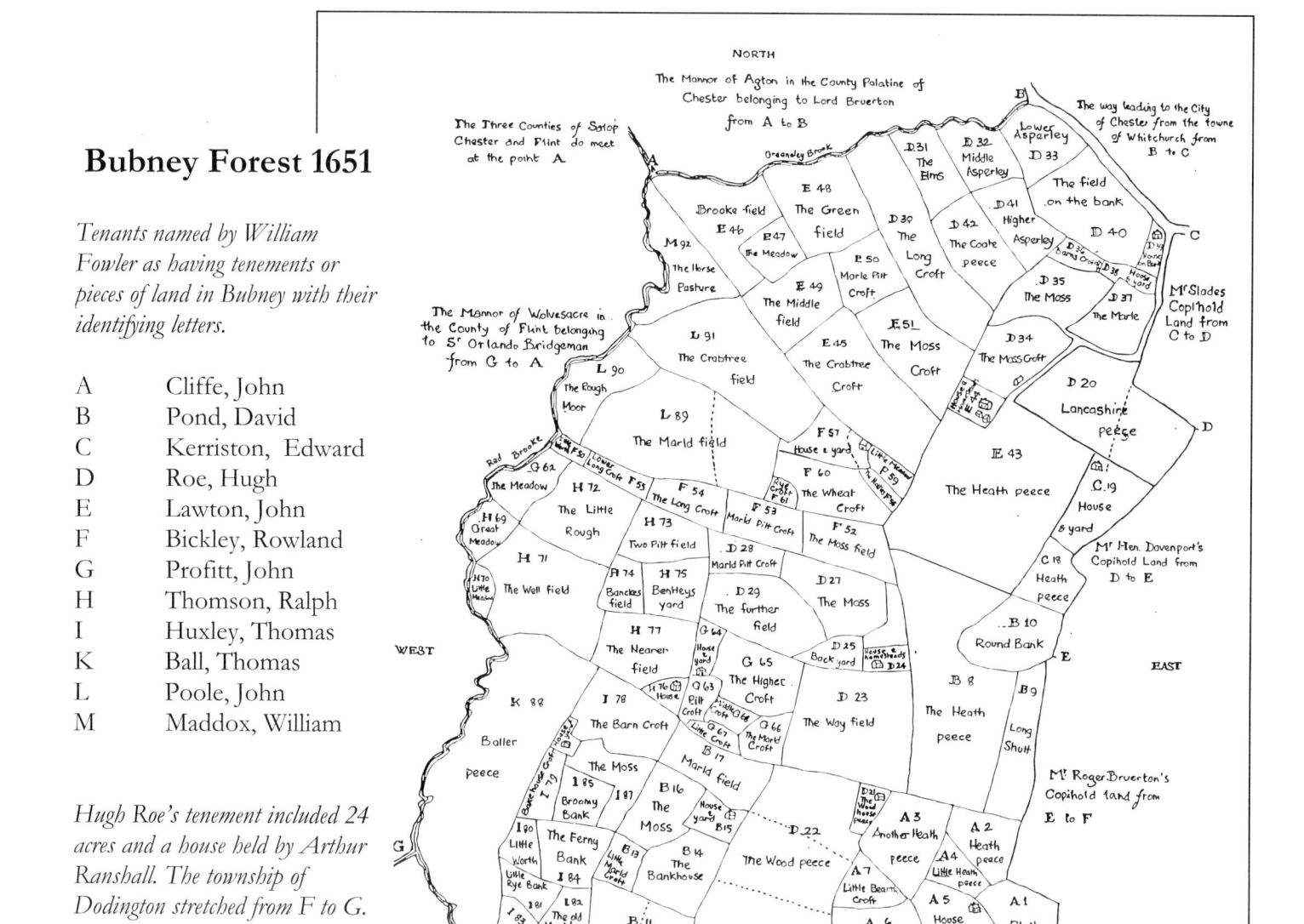

Tenants named by William Fowler as having tenements or pieces of land in Bubney with their identifying letters.

A	Cliffe, John
B	Pond, David
C	Kerriston, Edward
D	Roe, Hugh
E	Lawton, John
F	Bickley, Rowland
G	Profitt, John
H	Thomson, Ralph
I	Huxley, Thomas
K	Ball, Thomas
L	Poole, John
M	Maddox, William

Hugh Roe's tenement included 24 acres and a house held by Arthur Ranshall. The township of Dodington stretched from F to G.

'Dodington and Blackoe in the parish of Whitchurch' by William Fowler 1651c

This is an adaptation from the original plan produced by William Fowler. It brings together the field boundaries and names of their holders to show the extent of each person's farm. Also plotted are the approximate sites of farmhouses, or homesteads, noted in Fowler's schedule.

Capital letters refer to the schedule of property holders entered on the original map.

■ Homestead

The map of '*Dodington and Blackoe in the parish of Whitchurch*' – or rather of those parts leased out to 32 tenants – gave the same kind of information. Tenants were listed, fields named and acreages noted - just over 750 acres all told. Again, copyholders were indicated where their property abutted leased land, provided they too were in Whitchurch manor. Those over the national border in Flintshire were ignored. It is quite simple to recover the pattern of holdings and relate this, field by field, to much later maps, so accurate was Fowler's work. It is disappointing not to have information about land utilisation, but the large number of farms, all necessarily small, is most revealing about the degree of prosperity likely to have been enjoyed by those working this land. On average they had 26 acres apiece – a misleading figure as the range in Dodington was from 108 acres down to 1 acre, and only four men had more than 50 acres and thus a fair chance of earning a decent living. There were fourteen families with less than fifteen acres each.

Who were the people?

The people that Fowler probably met as he measured their fields and plotted their farmsteads are shadowy and difficult to bring to life. George Barnes, of all the property holders, is the only one who can be found in the diocesan probate lists up to 1671. It is probable that the John Larton, whose probate inventory was made in February 1662, was John Lawton of Bubney in the map schedule, and that Thomas Burrowes, whose probate was dated in May 1633, was the grandfather of Thomas Burrowes who had 108 acres in the Blackoe district of Dodington on the 1651 map. An Edward Profitt, whose probate date was in March 1634, may have been the father of John Profitt of Bubney in 1651, but as yet this is all very speculative.

George Barnes was not identified as a resident of Dodington by the appraisers of his personal property when they made an inventory on 29 October 1661. What they found in his possession at death, though, is consonant with him being the farmer recorded on the 1651 map. The Table below shows the items listed by Thomas Lovell and Thomas Nevett. Barnes worked 30 acres surrounding, but not including, an isolated part of Widow Bostock's Pan Castle holding. Thomas Nevett was his immediate neighbour, with a dwelling only a few yards away. An inventory of Nevett's goods at death in January 1674 suggests more questions than gives revealing information. Nothing more can be said about Barnes because his will doesn't now exist and there's no record of a burial at St. Alkmund's.

Was he a blacksmith? He had an anvil, billies and hammers and had done 3s 7d worth of 'smiths work' for John Barrow. He was also owed money by Samuel Simcock for 'shop work', and by six others for unspecified reasons. This is exactly the kind of list of customers to whom credit had been allowed by a tradesman, and found so often in probate inventories. Barnes would also seem to have been able to lend cash to others – perhaps the £2 in the hands of James Payne was such a loan. Equally, it might be classed more as a deposit with the nearest person locally who could be called a banker.

The surnames of all these people are familiar as seventeenth century inhabitants of the parish of Whitchurch at some time or other. One thing stands out from attempts at linking names together, however, and that is that the families of Whitchurch people were much more mobile than is often thought. The turn-over of the parish population was more rapid than many of us might expect.

	£	s	d
[Corrected total]	27	15	10
One cowe	3	0	0
One earelinge calfe	0	14	0
6 Earelinge sheepe	0	18	0
4 Lambs	0	8	0
Corne in the barne rye Barly payes	5	0	0
Haye	1	0	0
Wooll	0	10	0
An Anvill billyes and hammars and all tools	2	0	0
One Joyned bed & a chest	1	6	0
Tow payre of bedstockes and one truckell bed	0	6	0
Bedinge & ffurniture belonginge thereunto	3	0	0
3 brass potts	0	2	0
2 kettles and 1 skellett	0	16	0
9 pewter Dishes and some small pewter	0	10	0
Treanan wayre	0	12	0
1 grate and 1 brech and 1 peare of golberts 1 payre of pottracks pothookes and frying pan and 1 dreeping pan and 1 pare of belles	0	6	8
One table and 5 stools	0	10	0
2 ould cheeres	0	1	6
Benches and shilfes and 4 little Coffers	0	5	0
1 skrine	0	18	0
For his wayreinge Apparrell	0	15	0
Monnaye in James Paynes hands	2	0	0
Dett Dew from John Barrow for Smiths worke	0	3	7
Samuell Simcockes ffor shope weerke	0	16	11
Will Jarvice	0	1	7
Lawrance Hide	0	6	9
Will Burrowes	0	4	0
Mr Wicksted	0	10	11
Thomas Ranchall of grindley brooke	0	2	2
George Whittingham	0	11	9

George Barnes

This is a transcript of the inventory made for probate purposes on 29 October 1661. Those who listed and costed the value of George Barnes' goods and debts made an error in the addition which has been corrected. Also, the items have been rearranged in order of entry to bring those of a similar category together. Thus, household goods are grouped and kitchen possessions, for example, separated from beds and bed furniture. Money owed to Barnes is thrown into relief.

The original spelling has been retained, though this leaves a few terms which need to be pronounced with a local accent to understand! 'Payes' are peas; 'treanan' is treen or wooden ware, and 'skrine' is screen. 'Golberts' are iron bars or racks fixed so as to hold kettles or other cooking vessels over a fire.

The anonymous surveyor

A second set of maps of parts of the manor of Whitchurch survives. They were done in a different style from Fowler, and by a mapmaker unknown. Lands in at least seven of the townships were plotted by AS (the Anonymous Surveyor) in clusters, scattered widely and set out on paper sheets with little or no relationship to each other. His work duplicated Fowler's in only one instance – the district of Dodington township known as Blackoe. Like Fowler, AS indicated the names of tenants and identified the boundaries of their properties. He did not date his plans, however, nor did he give field names or acreages.

It is tempting to consider Daniel Rowley as AS. He was the man who helped Walter Fowler, junior, value William Fowler's possessions on death and must have known just what surveying instruments were worth because he was himself a mapmaker. Moreover, he made at least two maps for the second Earl of Bridgewater – one was part of Myddle and the other Kenwick Park, both in Shropshire - and signed them.[15] His technique and style were much more akin to Fowler's than to AS's, however, and it is difficult to see him, for example, working in one way in the 1630s or 1640s and quite another in the 1660s when he did the plans for the earl. Rowley and Fowler were closely allied, without doubt, with family roots fairly close geographically, living in the same part of Tettenhall parish

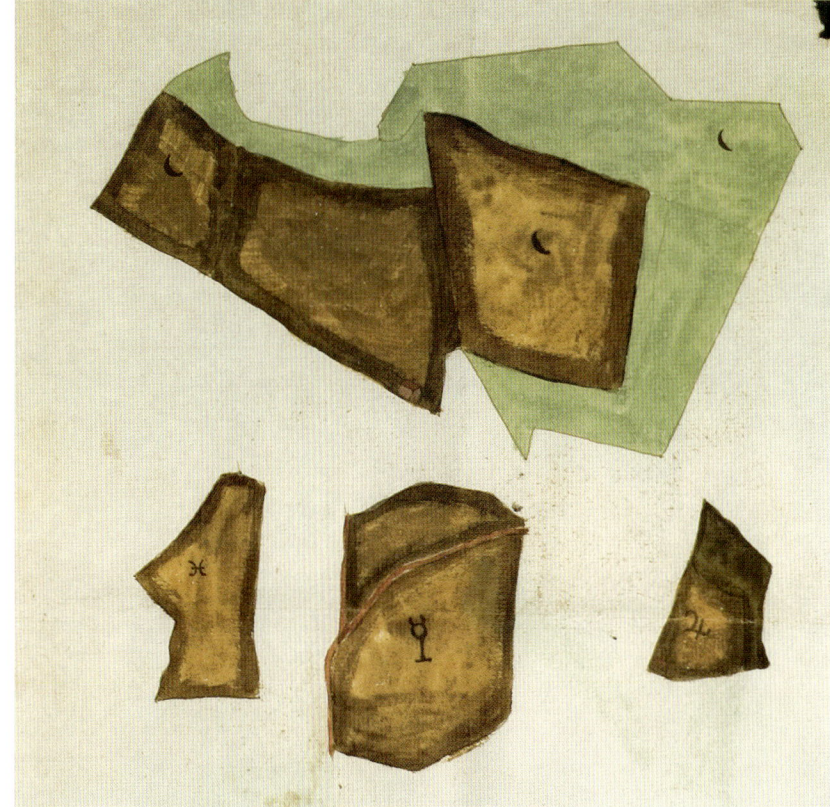

The Anonymous Surveyor

In the upper part of this one sheet of maps is Tilstock listed in the legend as in the tenure of Richard Newbracke. The three properties below, from left to right, are land at Broughall in the hands of Thomas Homfresonne, land at Edgley held by William Hodsonne and the third is a small piece of land in 'Duddingtonne' with 'Radulfe Burseys' as tenant.

in 1663, and having at least one employer in common.[16] In any case, given that Fowler was commissioned in 1651 when the Earl of Bridgewater had an urgent need to survey his properties, and that it is most unlikely that a surveyor was paid to work just on a whim, the anonymous maps should fit another occasion when a pressing requirement existed. This has to be before 1651 – the relatively primitive recording technique, amongst other things, suggests this – and the most obvious date would be in the late 1630s when the first Earl of Bridgewater at last had a chance to exert his authority over Whitchurch manor. This came on the death of his mother who had hitherto exercised lordship as part of her marriage settlement. Prior to that, the occasion for mapping the estate might have been 1617 when Thomas Egerton died and left his son to take on the estate and pick up the title of Earl of Bridgewater.

The only dating test as yet available for the anonymous maps is a series of manorial accounts for 1634, 1637 and 1641. This involves matching names of tenants on all maps and on rent rolls even though Fowler and AS only have the Blackoe district in common.

Blackoe names listed by AS are:- *Thomas Burrowes, Robert Burrowes, Rodger Maydley, Robert Jervase, Thomas Brama, John Loe, Xpofer Spenser, Richard Lee, Thomas Hamnett, John Birche, Thomas Brackes, WilliamRatcliffe, John Bedworth, Michael Atton, John Chessus, John Jenkin, Rodger Collin, William Ortonne, George Barlow, William Simpsonne, John Boswell.*

The only name AS and Fowler had in common in Blackoe was Thomas Burrowes. Both plotted virtually the same area for him. Otherwise, there were only three family names in common, Boswell, Lee and Spencer. Between the two dates there was obviously a considerable turn-over of tenants. The AS and 1641 rent roll lists are even more disparate, for Thomas Burrowes was not included in 1641 (William, Hugh and Richard Burrowes had separate holdings then) though the surnames of Boswell, Lee and Spencer occur with different Christian names in each case. The only significant, though tenuous, clues to dating the work of AS is the presence of Thomas Burrowes on his map, his absence in 1641 and then reappearance in 1651. It is known that a Thomas Burrowes of Dodington died in 1633.[17] If it is presumed that he was the grandfather of the 1651 Thomas, and the father of the three Burrowes listed in 1641, this would put the AS map before 1633 and suggest that it was the product of the first Earl inheriting his estate in 1617. In this case, it is no surprise that there was a considerable movement among the tenancies between 1617 and 1641: fourteen names listed by AS had disappeared by 1641. There was more stability in the 1640s as a comparison between the 1641 rent roll and Fowler's 1651 survey shows – but that's another story.

❧ *The Anonymous Surveyor's plan of 'Demeanes of Blackoe and Readiemore meadowe'* ❧

This has been edited to enhance the significant features hidden by the heavy colouring on the original. The original is one sheet of four in the collection of plans of parts of Whitchurch Manor. It is orientated with North on the left, but this has been changed to north at the top in the outline copy. The names of the tenants were separately listed in a Table, each given a symbol used on the plan to

The Anonymous Surveyor's plan of the *'Demeanes of Blackoe and Readiemore meadowe'*

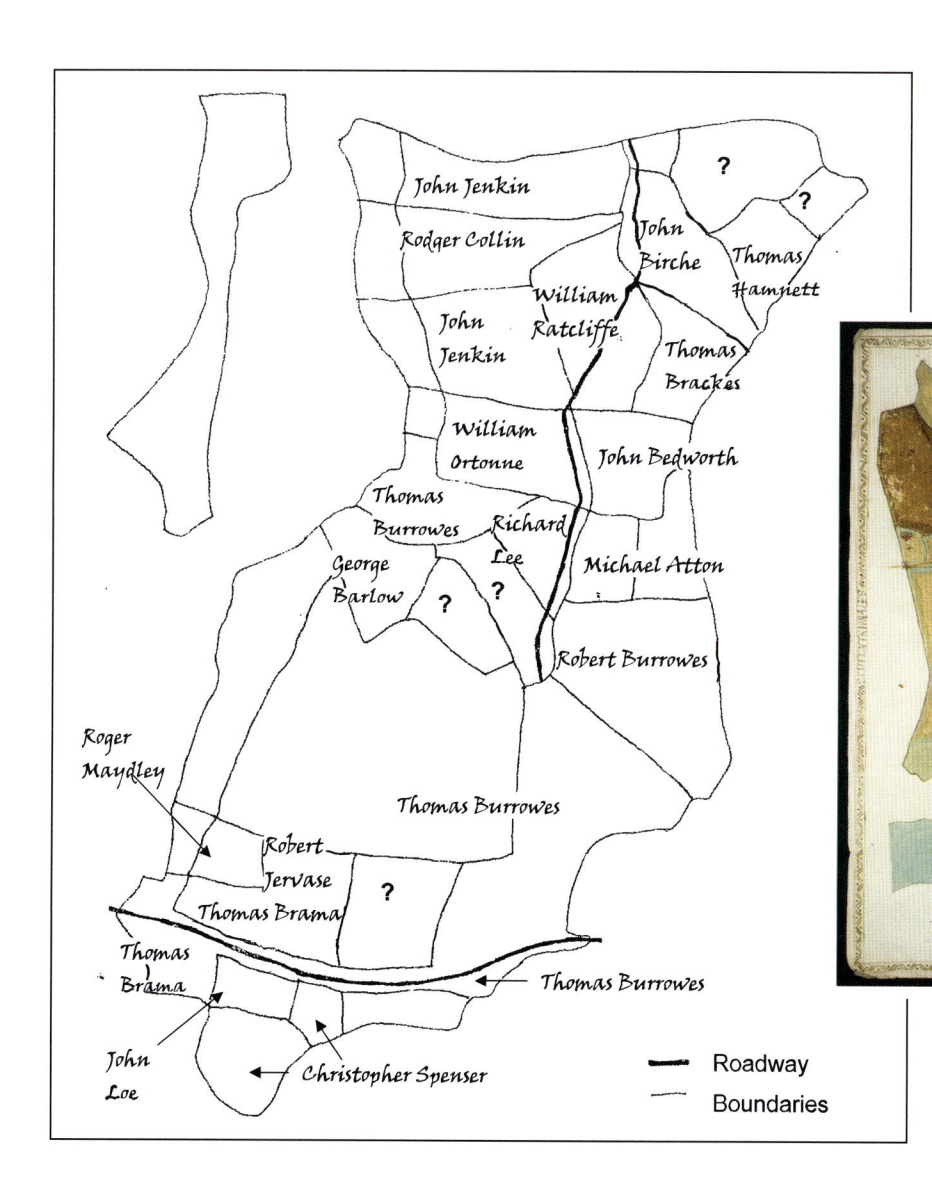

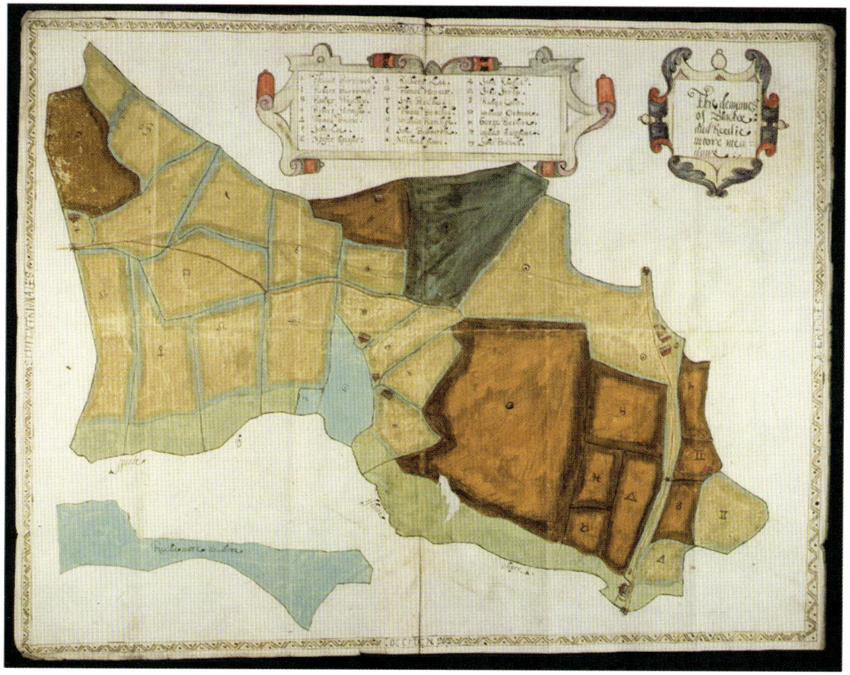

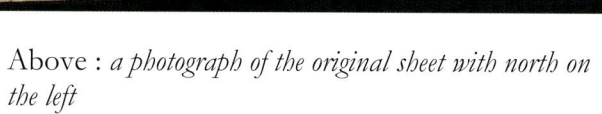

Above: *a photograph of the original sheet with north on the left*

Left: *an outline tracing of the property boundaries, with north at the top, showing the names of occupiers inserted where certainly known*

locate their property. In most cases the symbols are clear, but omitted here in favour of the names. Question marks indicate property of uncertain tenure.

There is no clue to the meaning of the colours used on the original, but two roads or trackways are evident and nine buildings are marked with house symbols. Alongside the main plan is 'Readiemore' which, in fact, should be placed immediately to the south of Christopher Spenser's holding and was presumably separated simply for convenience of using the available space on the sheet. There is no indication as to its status.

Other maps by the Anonymous Surveyor

AS clearly visited other leased lands in the manor. His simple field plans in different districts were drawn separately without being related to each other and were spread over three sheets. They can be seen now as a sheet within a framing border of farms in *'Oulde Woodhouse, Edgley, Broughehall, Little Ash, Tillstocke and Duddingtonne'*; a second sheet is but a fragment of what was a full map of *'Blackmeare Parke'*; and the third is only a part of Little Ash but, nevertheless, is a full plan inside a border. In each case the tenants were named and their fields identified by the use of pictorial symbols. The extent to which these plans can be related to field patterns drawn on later maps has not been tested, but the list of tenants is :-

Map 1. : 'Oulde Woodhouse, Edgley, Broughehall, Little Ash, Tillstocke, Duddingtonne'

Oulde Woodhouse *Ffardinando Richardsonne, Robert Hawkes*

Edgley *William Hodsonne*
Little Ash *Richard Gorstilloe*
Duddingtonne *Radulfe Burseys*
Tillstocke *Richard Newbracke*
Broughehall *Thomas Broughhall, Roger Hawkeshead, Thomas Greene, Thomas Homfresonne
The Catteralles*

Map 2 'Blackmeare Parke': *no tenants named*

Map 3 : Part of 'Little Ashe' *George (Sir) Manneringe (knight), Widdow Hughes, John Sempal, John Hughes and (blank), William Burgeis, William Bell, Widdowe Morall*

A plan of 'Tilstocke Park'

Another intriguing document is a plan, akin to those drawn by AS, but now assumed to be the work of a third surveyor, showing only *'Tilstock Park'*. It bears comparison with AS's sketch of land at Tilstock but is even more difficult to date. A modern writer on Shropshire landscape, Trevor Rowley, dates this single plan of Tilstock Park to the early seventeenth century, and it may well be that it is the first plan now available of that part of the manor of Whitchurch. Trevor Rowley's sketch plan (on the opposite page) is derived from the heavily coloured original and faithfully identifies all the important features.[18] It seems reasonable to suggest that it was a plan recording the enclosure of a former hunting area as subsequently leased out to three tenants, Green, Chawner and Gregorie. It remains a matter of speculation as to how this division of property into three is related to AS's identification of Richard Newbracke as the sole tenant.[19]

The map of Tilstock drawn by AS can be seen on page 51. It is the drawing in the upper part of the sheet with four distinct sections, one of which is green. Both this and the plan with three tenants are aligned with north on the left hand side. An argument can be made that when turned to a modern north-south orientation the location of the area can be found on more recent maps of Tilstock. On the Tithe Map 1841, for example, two Pool Meadows correspond with the pool copied by Trevor Rowley, and the pattern of roads is the same as that on the map of the enclosed park.

Strictly speaking, Tilstock, as part of Whitchurch manor, should be subject to further exploration. Local loyalties are such, however, that this village is thought to deserve separate consideration elsewhere. Similarly ignored for the moment is one other relevant sketch plan, undated, but possibly about 1598, which is used later to start a history of Whitchurch mills.

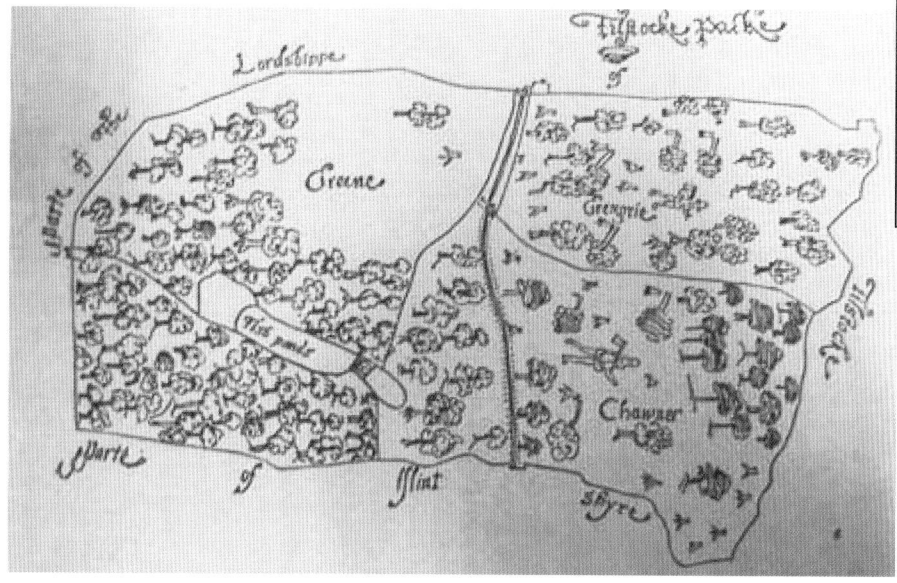

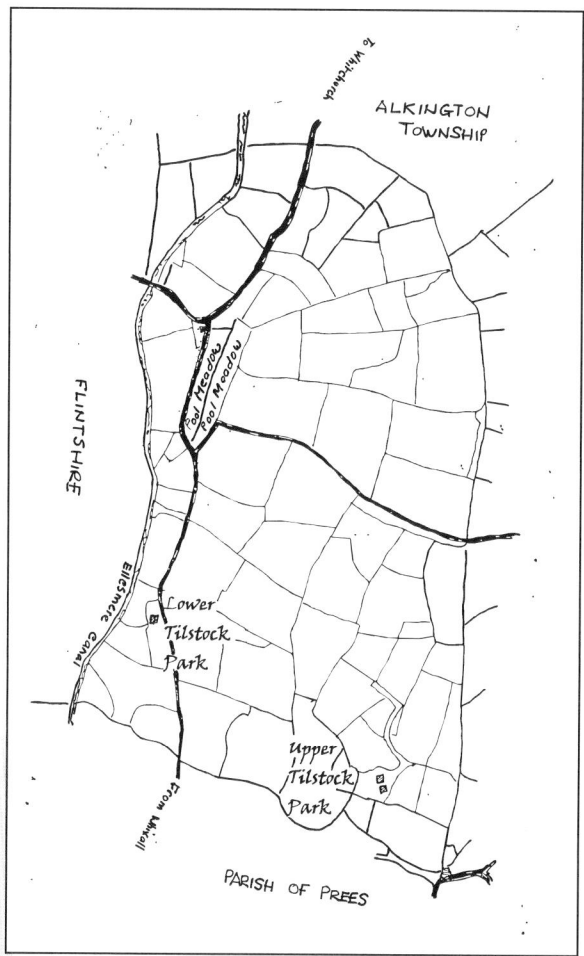

Left :
This is Trevor Rowley's copy of a map of Tilstock Park to reveal the details of the original which are almost totally hidden by dark green colour. It shows the Park as enclosed and divided between Chawner, Gregorie and Greene. If the supposed date of about 1600 is correct this is the earliest map of Bridgewater property.

Above : *The field and road pattern of the Tilstock Park area as shown on the 1839 Tithe Award map.*

End Notes

1. E. Hopkins, 'The Bridgewater Estates in North Shropshire in the first half of the seventeenth century' MA thesis University of London 1953 (hereafter Hopkins)
2. ShropA BP 212/Box 100 Survey of manor of Whitchurch 1641 by Richard Hyde and John Aldersey notes a property in Bubney as "surveyed by Mr Fowler"
3. *Transactions of Shropshire Archaeology Society*, XII (1900) article by Hon. Gilbert Vane on Matthew Fowler. This chapter relies also on A.D.M.Phillips 'The Staffordshire maps of William Fowler', in *South Staffordshire Archaeology and History Society* vol. 21 (1979-80) p15-24 (hereafter Phillips 1) and A.D.M. Phillips 'The seventeenth century maps and surveys of William Fowler' in *Cartographic Journal* vol. 17 (1980) p100-10
4. Phillips 1 p17 quoting National Library of Wales, Aberystwyth, PB 3065 and Lichfield Joint Record Office 1664 Probate Records [hereafter LJRO]
5. Phillips 1 p19. An IGI search suggests birth about 1613
6. Tettenhall Parish Register baptisms
7. Tettenhall Parish Register burial 'Sara uxor Gulielmi Fowler' : Phillips 1 p19
8. see footnote 3
9. James Hall, *History of town and parish of Nantwich* (1883) p180 quotes Malbon's Memorials for 1 March 1645 for a list of persons brought from Shrewsbury to be imprisoned in Nantwich. They include a "Doctor ffowler." Some moved to Manchester shortly after, and others were sent to Eccleshall Castle. On p 184 Hall quotes a list of all delinquents whose lands in Nantwich Hundred were sequestered. Among these was "Parson [Thomas] Fowler of Whitchurch, [Salop] ; noe order etc". In a footnote Hall states that Fowler was fined £130. [See Harl. M.S.2128] Presumably the property Thomas Fowler held was a wich house, for on p172 Hall quotes a Catalogue of Delinquents in Nantwich Hundred for whose lands Marc Folineux was responsible, where a "Mr Fowler" for "walling rents in Nantwich " paid £4-0-0. [See Harl. M.S. 2166]
10. Bernard Falk, *The Bridgewater Millions : a candid family history* (1942) p66 hereafter Falk
11. Falk op.cit p65-66
12. *Dictionary of National Biography*, John Egerton, second Earl of Bridgewater quoting *Cal. State Papers*, Dom 1651 p162
13. see Linda Peck *Consuming Splendour: Society and Culture in Seventeenth-Century England* (2005)
14. see the maps by mystery surveyor in ShropA 212 Box 466
15. Kenwick, ShropA 212 Box 466/D5 : Myddle 212/Box 466/21
16. P.Eden *Dictionary of Land Surveyors and Local Mapmakers* (1975) claims that Rowley did maps of estates in Staffordshire and Warwickshire as well as Shropshire, but this has not been substantiated.
17. LJRO probate. The inventory raises new questions because there were only eight entries for a few cooking utensils, one mare, bed coverings and wearing apparel - in total worth £5-19-0. Was he an old man who had passed on most of the proceeds of his 108 acre farm to his children? (Grateful thanks to Sylvia Watts for this information). It is possible that this is the Thomas Barrowes noted in a Survey of the manor of Whitchurch July 1634 who held a long lease on unspecified land dating back many years although he died the year before.
18. Trevor Rowley *The Shropshire Landscape* (1972)
19. John Gregory held a quarter of Tilstock Park in the 1637 manorial survey as did Arthur Wright (see Hopkins p165-7).

Whitchurch people in the 1630s

Maps of parts of Whitchurch in the seventeenth century refer to lots of names. The explorer into the history of the district cannot be certain that people listed as tenants on maps, or noted in the written surveys of the manor for that matter, actually lived on their property. It is more than likely that many did occupy what they leased – some undoubtedly sub-let the whole or part of their tenancies – but these lists are the best clue we have to the inhabitants of the place. At the very least, they usually tell us the name of the head of a family.

Three documents were drawn up so close together in date in the 1630s, noting property holders, that it is tempting to combine them as a means of getting to know more about the population at the time. Family historians won't easily find another way of locating Whitchurch ancestors at this date for the parish registers survive only from 1630. In any case, they only record in chronological sequence, burials, and, after 1633, christenings and marriages. They don't name the population as individuals all at the same moment. A census would do this, but there wasn't even a count made until 1801 and individuals were not named until 1841.

The three lists are not exactly comparable, two being surveys of the manor to note landholders and the conditions on which they leased property from the lord of the manor. The first in July 1634 was the responsibility of William Morton and the second was made in April 1637, but whether for precisely the same purpose as the earlier one is not entirely clear. [1] In both cases, however, the properties being investigated were probably, for the most part, not those lining the streets of the town itself. They were fields and closes, cottages and crofts in the surrounding rural area.

On the other hand, the third list of names, collected in 1636, was more than likely confined exactly to people who lived in houses closely packed together, either facing the principal streets or in the alleys and yards behind. [2] The objective of recording names was to make clear who was to supply various items of equipment required to fight fires. It may be assumed that the householders most at risk were the ones who had the responsibility for keeping easily available the buckets, ladders and hooks set against their names.

The combination of these lists of names is not an infallible way of finding out who lived in the manor in the mid-1630s. It is not even a guaranteed way of identifying all those who were the local social elite by virtue of occupying a house and land. The bulk of the inhabitants, we can be sure, were not so fortunate. There is, nevertheless, a strong indication here of just who was in the upper layer of Whitchurch society in the 1630s.

So far as possible double entries have been eliminated – that is to say where Christian names and surnames were exactly repeated in different lists, allowing for obvious variations in spelling, the second and subsequent entries have been excluded. The 1634 and 1637 lists are remarkably different with only about ten or twelve repeats of names. It seems certain that different types of tenants were being recorded in the two investigations. The overlap between names of fire equipment providers and people on the manorial surveys is also noticeably different. Perhaps nineteen cases at most of the same name can be identified. At least 71 people on the fire list did not appear in a manorial survey.

It would be possible to extend this search for names of persons who lived around the middle of the 1630s. One way potential members of the upper ranks of Whitchurch society might be found is to search probate records for the evidence of wills and inventories. A previous inquiry into these has been consulted but it adds only three names for the relevant period.[3] More names can be collected from parish registers, but there is no certainty as to individual social or economic status comparable with that found in the three lists used here.

There are great risks associated with drawing conclusions from a statistical analysis of the 192 people given here.[4] They were important enough to be recorded for what they held or had to do as individuals: in total, they are no guide to the size of the population of the manor or the town. More may be learnt about the property by recourse to the original documents, but acreages were absent, crops and livestock not reported and houses never described. Historical explorers are inured to disappointments arising from all the papers and artefacts they pore over : they rejoice at the richness of listings such as these found in three documents from the 1630s.

Extract from the 1636 Fire Equipment list

Mr Dudley	a longe hooke
William Wickstead	a leatherne bucket and a longe hooke
Mr ffiges widdow	a bucket and a longe hooke
Nathaniell Stockes	a brasen squirt and a longe hooke
Robert Richardson	a bucket and a Ladder
Thomas Broughall	a longe Hooke and a Ladder
ffrances Sanders	a bucket and a Ladder
Nathaniell Simcock	a longe hooke and a Ladder
John Kettle	a Bucket and a Ladder
Randall Judson	a Bucket and a Ladder

Note on the list which follows

Christian name and surname in one column are people from the combined 1634/37 list, with those italicised only in 1637. Christian name and surname in different columns are people in the fire equipment list.

Property holders in the 1630s in Whitchurch and Dodington townships, including Blackoe, but not Bubney

Name	1634/7	1636 Fire list	Address/status
Allen		William	
Balle, Thomas			Whitchurch
Barlowe, Alline			*Blackoe*
Barrow		John	butcher
Barrow		William	
Barrow		William	Junior
Barrowes, Thomas			Whitchurch
Bate, Joanne			Whitchurch
Beard		James	
Beddowes		Thomas and Edward	
Bell		John	
Bennyon		Roger	
Bentley		John	
Bickley, Rowland			Whitchurch
Bostocke		Thomas	
Bostocke			Widow
Boswell, John (now Thomas)			*Blackoe*
Brereton, Sir Thomas			Whitchurch
Brinley		Robert	
Bromfeild		Roger	
Bromhall, Robert			*Blackoe*
Brooke, Ellen			*Dodington*
Brookes		Elizabeth	Mrs
Broughall		Thomas	
Broughall		Robert	
Bryan			Widow
Buckley		John	
Bunbey		Wilfrey	
Burche, Henry			*Blackoe*
Burges, Robert [Bridges ?]			*Dodington*
Burghall, Thomas : heir to George Burghall			Dodington
Burrowes, Hugh			*Blackoe*
Burrowes, Richard			*Dodington*
Burrowes, William (now Richard)			
Carrier, Randull			Whitchurch
Cawley, [?]			
Chessowes, Thomas			*Blackoe*
Chetall		Roger	
Cliffe		Allen	
Clowes, John			Dodington
Clyffe, John			Whitchurch
Colefax		George	
Constantine, Thomas (aged 8 yrs) heir to William Constantine gent			Dodington
Constantine, William		*heirs of*	*Dodington*
Cooper		Allen	
Cooper Thomas			Whitchurch
Corbishley, Robert			Dodington
Cotton, Phillipp			
Cowper, Allen			
Crewe, Randull			Whitchurch
Croxton, Hugh			Whitchurch
Curbachley, Robert			Dodington
Deaves, Anne widow			Dodington
Dicken		Thomas	
Dickinson, Caroline			Whitchurch
Dodd, Anne widow			Dodington
Downe, Arthur			
Downes Adam			Whitchurch
Dudley			Mr

59

Name	1634/7	1636 Fire list	Address/status
Eaton		Hugh	
Eddow, Roger			Whitchurch *also Blackoe*
Edge		Thomas	
Evan, William			Whitchurch
Evans, Edward			Whitchurch
Evans, Richard			
ffairboro		Thomas	
ffiges		Mr	widow
ffiges, Jesabell widow			Dodington
ffiges, Susanna [also John]			Whitchurch
Garrett Thomas			Whitchurch
Gill, John			*Blackoe*
Gittens, Ellinor wife to John Gittens joint heiress to John Merrick			Dodington
Gregory, William			
Griffith Ursula			Whitchurch
Grindley, James (& Higginson, Alice)			Dodington
Grindley, William			Whitchurch
Hamner, William			
Hamnett, John			*Blackoe*
Hankinson James			Whitchurch
Hankinson, Amye widow and Thomas Hankinson her son			
Hardinge, Randle			
Hassard		John	
Hickson		William	
Hide, Richard			Blackoe
Higginsonn		Richard	
How		Richard	
Howell		John	
Hupkin		John	
Hurd, Roger			*Blackoe*
Hurleston, Thomas			Whitchurch
Huxley, Thomas			Whitchurch
Huxley, William			Whitchurch
Hynton, Jane widow of William			*Whitchurch*
Jackson		Robert	
Jarvis, William			*Blackoe*
Jellico		Thomas	
Jenkin, Owen		alias Davyes	Whitchurch
Jenks		John	
Jenkyn		David	
Judson [?], Randle			
Kettle, John			
Kettle, William			*Blackoe*
Larton Elizabeth			Whitchurch
Latemore		Robert	
Lavell		John	
Lea William			Whitchurch
Lea, Ellen widow			Dodington
Leech		Raph	
Leech			Widow
Leech, John			
Lightfoote, Thomas			*Blackoe*
Llewelin, Allin			
Lloyd		Leonard	
Lovell, Thomas			Dodington
Lowes		Thomas	
Maidely, Ellen			*Blackoe*
Manchester, William			Blackoe
Medcalffe George			Whitchurch
Meredyth, Roger			*Blackoe*
Merrick, John			Dodington
Merrick, William			Dodington
Merrike, Allin			Whitchurch
Minshall, Alline			
Morehall, Alice			Whitchurch
Mossis, George			Dodington
Nevett, Jane			
Nevett, John			Dodington
Nevitt ?		Richard	Shoemaker
Nevitt ?		Thomas	Tanner
Painter		John	
Pawley, William			Dodington
Payne		Richard	
Payne		James	
Pearesall		John	

Name	1634/7	1636 Fire list	Address/status
Penkethman			Widow
Poole, John heir to Roger Poole			Dodington
			Whitchurch
Probin, Randle			Dodington
Probyn, Edward			
Purefoy, Raph (clerk)			Dodington
Pursell William			Whitchurch
Ranshall	Thomas		
Reade	Allen		
Rhodes	Thomas		
Richardson, Robert & Whittfield, Joshua			
"and the rest of the shoe makers of Whitchurch"			
Riley	Robert		
Rowley	Humphrey		
Roycrofte	Lawrence		
Salmon	Raph		
Sanders	ffrancces		
Sanders	William		
Sandford	John		gent
Sarr, Jane wife to John Sarr, joint heiress to John Merrick			Dodington
Savage, John			Dodington
Shone	Thomas ap		
Simcock	Nathaniell		
Simcoke	Samuell		
Socklidge	John		
Stockes	Nathaniell		
Spenncer, John			*Blackoe*
Swift, Robert			Whitchurch
Swinerton	Raph		
Symcoke	John		
Symson, John his widow			Dodington
Symson, Thomas			Dodington
Tabott	Richard		
Tatnall	George		
Tompson William			Whitchurch
Turner	Richard		
Turnor, Richard			
Weecksteed Katherin			Whitchurch
Welch	Thomas		
Welch	Raph		Junior
Welsh, Ralph			Dodington
Wenlowe or Wenloxe	Richard		
Whitehall, Richard			Dodington
Whitfeild	Joseph		
Whitingham, Richard			
Whittingham	George		
Wickstead	Anna		widow
Wickstead, [?]			
Wickstead, William			
Wicksted, Thomas,			Dodington
Wilkinson, James			
Willaston	Arthur		gent
Wright, John			Dodington
Wynne			Mr

****

End Notes

1. 1634 Survey in ShropA 212 Box 346/19 : 1637 Survey in ShropA 212 Box 346 (20/2)
2. ShropA 212 Box 59 (a)
3. See the transcripts of inventories for Whitchurch in the 1630s by Sylvia Watts held at LJRO.
4. 186 entries with at least six other people coupled with the principal name

Burials in families affected by plague 1650-51

William Andrew
Margery Baker, Jone Baker, Anne Baker, Anne Baker
Elizabeth Braddock, Elenor Braddock, Thomas Braddock
Anne Burch
Ellen Burrow
Allen Burrows, Ellen Burrowes,
John Clark
Alles Colefax, George Colefax, Anne Colefax, Nathaniel Colefax, Arthur Colefax
Mary Cooke
Susanna Cooper, William Cooper, Anne Cooper, Dorothy Cooper, Thomas Cooper, Jane Cooper, David Cooper
Thomas Davies
Margery Edge, Margaret Edge, Arthur Edge, Elizabeth Edge
Dorothy Evanes
Sarah Fell, John Fell, Rebecka Fell
Margaret, Figes, John Figes
Mary Figis
Elizabeth Gill
Margery Griffiths, Elenor Griffiths
Mary Harper
John Hayward, a child Hayward, Elizabeth Hayward
Ellen Houlbrook
William Huxley, Margery Huxley, William Huxley, William Huxley
Margaret Jelfes
Charles Iseson, Ellen Iseson
John Jenkin, Margery Jenkin, William Jenkin
John Jennings, Elenor Jennings
Thomas Lea, Jonathan Lea
Jane Leech
Margaret Miles
John Moore, Sarah Moore, William Moore, a child Moores (?)
John Morhall, Alles Morhall
Hugh Morris
A child Nevet, a child Nevet, William Nevet
Alles Newman, Peeter Newman, James Newman
Katherine Newton
Mary Owen
William Parker
Margaret Peeres
Thomas Poole, Isabell Poole, Edward Poole
Mary Ranshall, Alles Ranshall, Mary Ranshall, William Ranshall, Joanne Ranshall, Thomas Ranshall
Elizabeth Rogers, Thomas Rogers
Mary Shorter
Randle Stokes
Gwen Titley
William Tomson, Margaret Tomson
Thomas Weaver
Henery Weaver, Sarah Weaver
Alles Whitbey
Anne Williams, Ellen Williams, John Williams, Thomas Williams
Samuel Williams
Thomas Wright, John Wright, Samuel Wright, John Wright, Thomas Wright, Margaret Wright, Margery Wright, a child Wrights

The Plague in Whitchurch 1650-51

In the summer of 1650, eighteen months after the execution of King Charles I and at almost the same time that William Fowler was measuring fields in Dodington, Whitchurch was struck by plague. The outbreak was so severe that the Parish Clerk wrote in the Register of Burials that plague appeared on 2 August and "those persons who died thereof are marked + before their names." Of the total of 131 burials between August 1650 and May 1651 there were 113 marked the result of plague. Of these, almost half were children, for the Register shows that 28 men, 30 women and 55 children died of the plague during that time.[1] The clerk's note is a certain sign that the community was deeply affected not so much by an increase in numbers of deaths but by the especially frightening nature of the disease. It is just this kind of remark in a parish register which excites the interest of the historical explorer.

Plague, recognised from swellings in the lymphatic glands known as 'buboes', a common symptom of the disease, had been endemic in England since the mid-fourteenth century. The first deadly epidemic, known as the Black Death, from the bruises caused by haemorrhage under the skin, had fearful results all over the country. In Whitchurch manor the effects were devastating. Rich and poor suffered alike. W. J. Slack, in his *History of Agriculture in North Shropshire* stated that "an Inquisition Post-Mortem of 1349 shows that John le Strange (the Lord of the Manor) and his son Foulke both died of the pestilence". In the adjoining township of Dodington, he goes on, 'there are two carucates of land which were not worth 6s yearly … the jurors do not know how to extend the said land because the domestic and labouring servants there are dead and no one is willing to hire the land. The water mill is sunk from 30s to 6s 2d because the tenants are dead.'[2]

In 1650, however, the consequences of the outbreak of plague in Whitchurch were not so disastrous. Of an estimated parish population of 2,500, evidence from the Churchwardens' Accounts indicates that the majority lived in the urban areas of Whitchurch and Dodington. The 113 people who died were about 5% of the total population, and it is probable that most of these had lived in the town.

After the plague broke out in early August it spread rapidly for three months. In July there had only been 4 burials, but in August there were 21, doubled to 43 in September, declining to 32 in October. In September there were two funerals almost every day except Sundays. By November and December the death rate had dropped sharply to 11 and 12, and in the early months of 1651 to the more usual rate of 4 or 5 a month. Two or three of these died of plague. The last recorded plague burials were those of Jane, daughter of Robert Leech, and William, son of Thomas Jenkin, in early May 1651. The suddenness of the onset and concentration of burials in three months before winter properly set in are two striking characteristics inviting speculation about the type of affliction which gave the parish clerk so much concern.

Towns all over England had suffered from sporadic attacks of what was known as 'plague' for three hundred years since 1349. In the Midlands, Leicester had as many as ten episodes between 1564 and 1639. Worcester suffered almost as badly with seven recorded outbreaks. Nantwich in 1603, Dudley in 1617, Stafford 1640, Lichfield 1646-7 and Chester 1647 all suffered before 1650, when Shrewsbury was afflicted. More than 300 people died there between June and October. It is probable that the disease spread from Shrewsbury to Whitchurch, twenty miles to the north, in the summer of 1650. The infection took six weeks to travel which, according to J. F. D. Shrewsbury in his book *Bubonic Plague in the British Isles,* is consistent with its spread by rats carrying particularly virulent fleas. [3]

The common term 'plague' for an epidemical disease was used in the ages before scientific knowledge was acquired. Causes could not be identified and cures were wild speculations. Recent investigations into descriptions of symptoms, the pattern of plague burials and the distributions of rat populations show that the once popular theory of a single disease the product of bites by fleas peculiar to black rats is scientifically dubious.[4]

Epidemics of frightening proportions with horrible effects on those who were infected certainly happened; none of the remedies recommended by physicians could prevent the spread or relieve the symptoms. There was a distinct, and in the seventeenth century, well-known history of epidemics occurring many times in the past and a recognition that governments had a duty to act to confine the incidence to as small an area as possible. One way was to legislate for parishes to build pesthouses into which the sick were incarcerated; another was to enforce a quarantine zone with no entry or exit allowed. Among the rules was that commanding parish clerks to identify those who were buried after death from the disease. It is this record which as much as any other evidence is the clue to the exact nature of each specific epidemic, including the method by which disease spread. Studies of parish registers, in other words, have provided modern scientists with the clues they need to challenge the description of plagues from the Black Death onwards as being 'bubonic', or rat-carried diseases.

Of the 51 families affected in Whitchurch, 24 lost only one person. Of the remaining 27 families, nine suffered the most severely with four or more persons dying from the plague. The first one to succumb was Margery Edge who was buried on 3 August; she was followed by her daughter Margaret on 6 August. Four other relatives died during the next four months. On 6 October William Cooper was buried, followed by his sisters Anne and Dorothy on the 7th and 8th, their father Thomas on the 11th and then their sister Jane and brother David on the 28th and 29th. The Ranshall family also suffered badly, losing six members between 28th October and 14th December. It is impossible to know why some families suffered much more severely than others, but it is possible that the advice about hygiene and quarantine sent out by the Privy Council in 1636 may have had some effect.

The real cause of the disease was unknown at this time, but experience had shown that the infection spread most rapidly in crowded communities. The Order of the Privy Council issued in London in 1636 gave advice by the College of Physicians "containing certain necessary Directions as well as for the cure of the Plague, as for preventing the Infection; with many easie Medicines and of small charge, the use whereof may be profitable to his Majesties Subjects". The advice included quarantine for people or goods coming from suspected places, when "they should be put to the pest house or some such like place for fourty daies - (according to the custom of Italy)". It was realised also that hygiene was important in the fight against plague. The sale of "corrupt flesh or fish" was forbidden. "Scavengers in general and in every particular house holden [should] take care for the due and orderly cleansing of the streets and private houses which will avail much in this case. … Doggs, Catts, Conies and tame Pidgeons [should] be destroyed about the Towne ….. and that no Swine be permitted to range up and down the streets as they frequently do, rather not to keep any at all." When a household was found to be infected no person was to be allowed to leave it, "though none be dead therein, to be shut up and carefully kept watched by more trusty men than ordinary warders till a time after the partie be well-recovered, and that time to be fourty days at the least." [5]

These regulations were meant primarily for London and other large towns, but they do show that efforts were made to prevent the spread of infection. They also demonstrate, according to the most recent historical inquiries, that there was an established recognition that the plague was passed from person to person, encouraged by dirty living spaces more than likely, and not caused by infestations of rats.

Clearly, it was not only the poor who suffered. The names of those who died in Whitchurch include some who were well-known in the town during the seventeenth century. The names of Cooper, Jenkyn, Colefax and ffiges appear in the list of those who had to provide fire-fighting equipment under the Bye-Laws of 1636, while a Thomas Ranshall and Thomas Edge were among the Jurors who put their names to the Bye-Laws. Later, between 1655 and 1680, copyhold property surrenders and the Eddowes Survey of 1667 mention the names ffiges, Cooper, Ranshall, Edge, Burrowes and Hayward. [6] All these names appear in the Register of those who died of plague in 1650-51. It is probable that nearly all lived in the town centre. For example, in 1667 an Arthur Cooper was the occupier of the Raven Inn in High Street, as had been his father before him, and William ffiges surrendered two houses in High Street, one being the Red Lion Inn (later the Victoria Hotel) in 1671. [7] This suggests that the plague in Whitchurch was not confined to the very poor, but that the better-off families of inn-keepers and merchants also suffered.

Towards the end of the century the plague disappeared from England. The most famous (because the best documented) episode after the Black Death was the Great Plague of London in 1665. It was the last major outbreak in this country. Several reasons for the disappearance of plague can be found in popular historical literature. G. M. Trevelyan in *English Social History* and Jeremy Lake in *The Great Fire of Nantwich* both suggest that the increase in the number of brick-built houses and the replacement of straw floor covering and cloth wall-hangings by carpets and wood panelling may have reduced the number of rats and fleas which were harboured by the older timber-framed wattle and daub buildings. [8] Trevelyan also quoted a theory that the elimination of the medieval black rat by the 'modern' brown rat, which is not a carrier of the plague flea, is a more likely cause of the decline of the disease.

The most plausible accounts now argue that the identification of *bubonic* plague as caused by rat fleas biting humans may be acceptable, but the Black Death and the Great Plague of 1665, together with all the plagues in between, were not bubonic at all. There were symptoms in skin degeneration in common with bubonic plague which frightened all observers, but they have misled medical historians into seeing only one type of plague when in fact there were two. The form which came to Whitchurch in

1650 was noted by the most thorough-going writer of the bubonic school, J.F.D.Shrewsbury, as spread by packs of rats moving about the country. He could cite no evidence for this phenomenon other than the incidence of the disease itself. Analyses of many parish recordings of burials of plague victims, however, produce a pattern of times and dates in conflict with any possible rat journeys, thus leaving open the question of ultimate origin of a disease now taken to be viral in type. It was movement of individuals which infected new victims, with the length of the period of incubation before the appearance of the dreaded symptoms under arms and in groins, followed rapidly by death, which is the crucial clue to how plague was transmitted. Thanks to the meticulousness of numerous parish officials – probably Thomas Porter, the Presbyterian interloper, in the case of Whitchurch – local historians have the chance to investigate the nature of a puzzling feature in the development of their communities in the light of the latest scientific knowledge. [9]

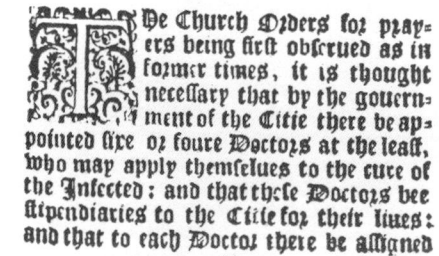

End Notes

1. There is some slight confusion over exact numbers, two counts by other people result in totals also of 112 and 117. There is also a small variation in the number of burials in the same period of people not identified as plague victims – 22 as against the figure here of 18.
2. The publication details have not been found
3. J.F.D. Shrewsbury, *A History of Bubonic Plague in the British Isles* (1970)
4. S.Scott & C.Duncan, *Biology of Plagues* (2001) : S.Scott & C.Duncan, *The Return of the Black Death: the world's greatest serial killer* (2004)
5. College of Physicians *Certain Directions for the Plague* (1636)
6. For 1626 Bye Laws see ShropA 212 Box 59 (a); for Eddowe's Survey of 1667 see ShropA 212 Box 108
7. For occupiers of property see R.B. James, *Old Inns of Whitchurch* (1984) p2, 17
8. G.M.Trevelyan, *English Social History* (1946); Jeremy Lake, *The Great Fire of Nantwich* (1983) p98
9. For a full account of the latest research into the plague in Britain and Europe see the works by S. Scott and C. Duncan already quoted.

The Duke of Bridgewater's Whitchurch estates 1761

The Duke of Bridgewater had been in France in 1754 and seen the future. He was the Duke popularly called 'the Canal Duke', and the waterway named after him linking Manchester to Liverpool is, somewhat misleadingly, considered the first major transport improvement of the Industrial Revolution. It was a costly business investing in huge civil engineering projects such as long-distance canals, but by 1760 the young Francis Egerton, third Duke of Bridgewater, was taking a leading role in promoting new canals of an hitherto undreamed of length. He had seen the Canal du Midi and therefore knew what could be done. [1]

Francis Egerton, as a younger son, was not regarded by his mother as a likely head of the family, but his brother's death gave him the title and estate at the age of twelve. His relatives thought his education needed careful management so he was sent abroad for over two years in the care of a tutor. This did not altogether prevent him from leading a colourful life, to the despair of his guardian, and after returning and claiming his rights in 1757, at the age of twenty-one, his style of living did not much alter. Despite strenuous attempts he failed to find a wife, and by 1760 he had deliberately turned to estate management and canal building as an alternative to society life. His reputation as an aristocrat was for relative poverty, although in his lands there was huge potential for wealth.

This was certainly the occasion, and maybe the cause, of commissioning George Grey to survey all his estates in the manor of Whitchurch. [2] He needed to value his assets and determine his financial base. Just what Bridgewater took from Grey's maps and reports is difficult to establish, but to the historical explorer of North Shropshire they are invaluable. For one thing, they allow direct comparisons to be made for parts of the district with the maps drawn a century before by William Fowler, and those even earlier by an anonymous mapmaker.

George Grey and his maps

George Grey of Lancaster dated his survey of the manor of Whitchurch in 1761. He produced one extremely large map giving an over-view of the whole manor, and a bound book of plans of individual parts with a separate field register. His work showed field boundaries and lists of tenants whose holdings he plotted on the maps with the acreage each held. As with Fowler a century earlier, Grey was apparently instructed to ignore copyhold lands, but there is no indication as to the terms on which the farms recorded on the maps were held. He did indicate land use, however, on the single large map, differentiating between pasture, meadow, and arable as well as water, woodland and farmsteads. His cartographical standards were equal to the highest of his day, and the result is a rich resource for the local historian.

Grey is not a surveyor about whom there is extensive knowledge. In fact, almost nothing is known, although he also produced a map of the Duke's headquarter estate of

Ashridge.[3] It has been claimed that he made maps of parts of estates in Derbyshire and Cheshire, as well as in Lancashire, but evidence has not been found to substantiate this.[4] The mystery is that the properties the Duke was intent on developing were in Lancashire, and the canals he envisaged to carry coal and other bulk materials had to be meticulously planned. Grey does not seem to have been employed in this capacity at all. Neither were there estate maps of Worsley, for example, where the Duke had his coalmines, nor maps of his Cheshire estates or of Ellesmere in Shropshire. It's a nice question why Whitchurch was singled out for this treatment.[5]

The single large map covering the whole manor has been copied in outline to display how scattered were the groups of farms and single properties outside the town's streets, and to highlight the five largest blocks of property from which the Duke drew income. It is this degree of selectivity that suggests that the particular types of holdings plotted excluded copyhold. Grey calculated that there were 5,913 acres shared between the 169 individuals on his list of tenants. He counted Whitchurch Heath, Brown Moss, Blakemere and Osmere as well as other bits of waste and the lanes in this total. A check on his figures produces a few questions and a total of about 5,100 acres of tenanted land – an average of about 31 acres per tenant.

Black Park was the largest single aggregation of property with just over 1,260 acres between eighteen tenants. J.Fallows had the second largest farm in the manor here with approximately 298 acres. Little Ash ranked second in size as a block and had the largest farm of some 361 acres, held by H.J.Gregory. There were some 650 acres surveyed by Grey in Dodington, just over 425 acres in Bubney, 224 acres in Blackoe and over 811 acres in Tilstock. The map is somewhat misleading as to the nature of land distribution in Tilstock as a look at the schedule of tenants shows. This was a township where there were many tenants – 52 in fact – but most had tiny properties too small to show up on the map of the whole estate. There were two farms over 100 acres and another four over 50 acres, but fifteen people had less than an acre apiece, and nineteen more had less than ten acres. Overall, the Duke had over 811 acres let out on some form of tenancy but the district contrasted sharply with other townships in that there was considerable subdivision of land here. The same could be said of Whitchurch township, but the urban settlement accounted for the high proportion of tenants with less than an acre. Tilstock had not evolved as a retail centre or site for professionals doing business.

The townships of least value for the Duke were Great Ash, where W. Hughes was the only significant tenant, and the two Woodhouses, where again small-holdings predominated, all-told hardly exceeded 81 acres. The Duke had little in Alkington and in Broughall, but at least E.Wood had a farm in the former with some 63 acres.

The book of maps contains more detailed plans of each district outlined on the large manor map. Very close examination is possible, farm by farm, of all the holdings, with fields named and measured. A separate index conveniently lists tenants in alphabetical order and identifies their fields. Unfortunately, there are some discrepancies between these plans and names of tenants and the information recorded on the large map. In the case of Black Park these are hardly of great import, but there are puzzles in Dodington. Questions which naturally arise are not only why this was so, but which particular piece of information should be taken as relevant. The map details and names reported here are all derived from the

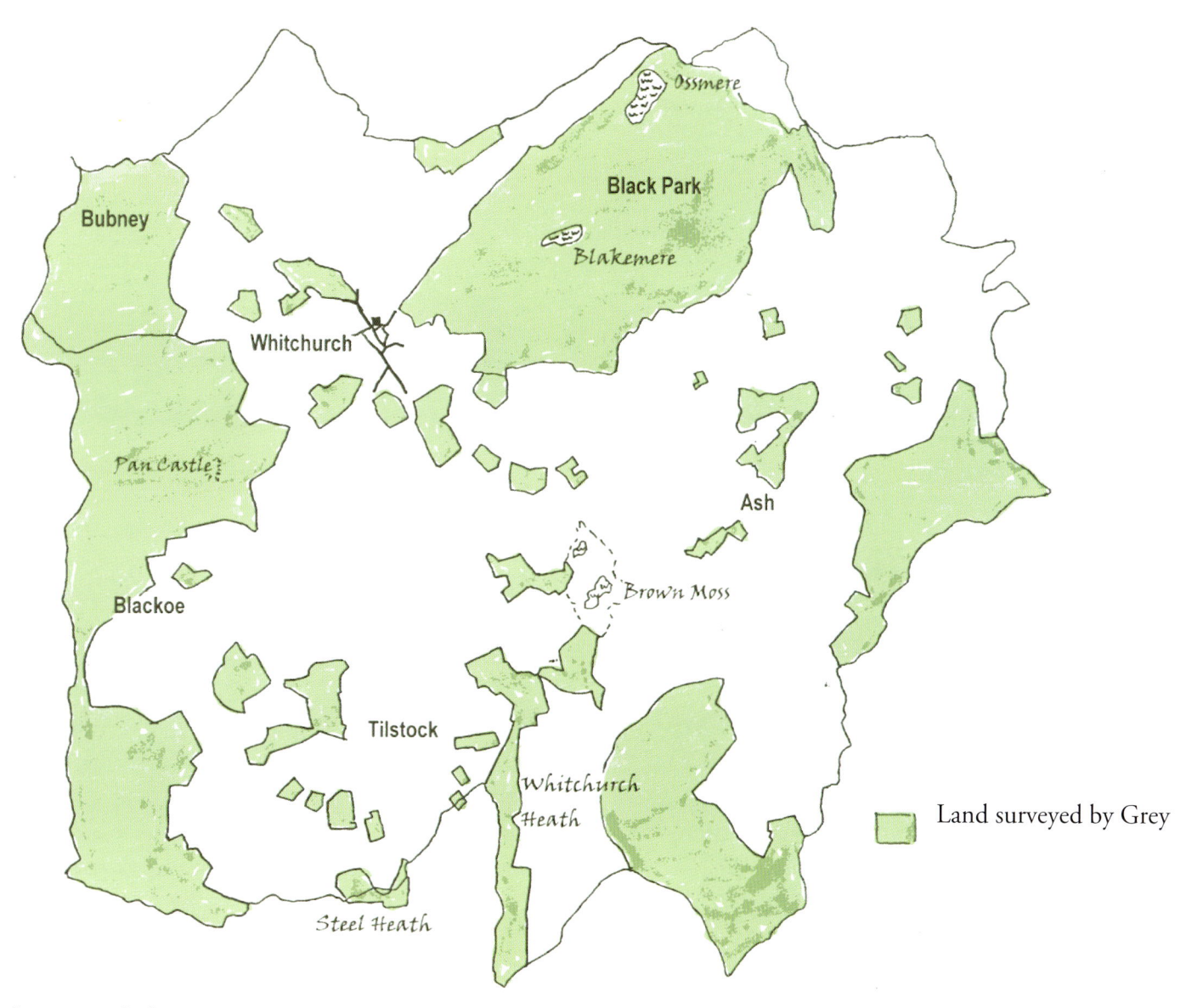

Areas of the manor of Whitchurch surveyed in 1761 by George Grey

large single map of the whole manor. In part, this is because more information over-all is available from that source, and, secondly, for the sake of consistency. All these maps are dated 1761. There is no hint that they represent different times of the year, and therefore changes in tenants after, say, Lady Day or Michaelmas.

There are no clues to categories of lease or conditions of tenancy, and certainly no information about rents, crops, soil types or the state of the land. All sections of the work are meticulously presented without any suspicion that one part was preparatory to the other. For the moment, it has to be sufficient to take note of differences - where they seem worth consideration - and accept that no quick answers are apparent to the historian's inevitable queries.

The town plan and account of urban tenancies reveal just how few plots of land and houses the Duke still held outside copyhold. This has had separate examination in an earlier chapter.

ᔕ Changes since the mid-seventeenth century ᔕ

A study of the Egertons' interest in, and degree of success with, estate management in the mid-eighteenth century could be most interesting, especially in comparison with the efforts of other aristocrats. In the case of Whitchurch some limited conclusions can be drawn about at least one issue of significance – the pace of change in the size of farms. A closer look at the areas which William Fowler had previously surveyed – Dodington and Bubney – is

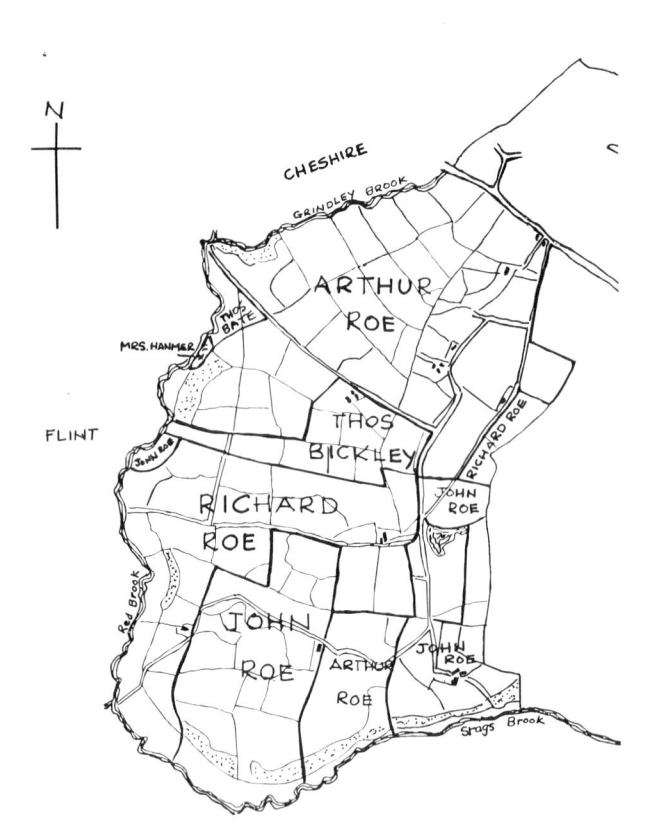

1761 Map of Bubney farms and their occupiers
compiled from the original map by George Grey

necessary for this purpose. Grey's survey covered the manor in its entirety so that all the townships were dealt with in the same way. The extent to which a reduction in the number of tenants and an enlargement of individual holdings over a century can only be measured, however, from two of these districts, but this is not a negligible test. Other evidence is required to discover whether change was deliberate policy or not.

Bubney farms changed in size and location but not entirely in families holding leases. The obvious development since 1651 was the virtual take-over of the ground by the Roe family. Three of them held 396 acres whereas their ancestor, Hugh, had leased only a fraction of that total – field measurements have not been taken from Fowler's map. Broadly speaking, Hugh's 1651 farm had descended to Arthur Roe, while John and Richard Roe had come in to take more or less all the rest, with one significant exception. The Bickley farm held by Rowland in 1651 was the same as that held by Thomas Bickley in 1761. In other words, whereas twelve tenants divided Bubney between them in 1651, by 1761 this number had been reduced to five, and three were of one family. Whether by accident or design, farm territories had increased in Bubney over a century, but two families had maintained their place.

In Dodington and Blackoe the jigsaw of land holdings was more complicated, and yet had simplified over the century

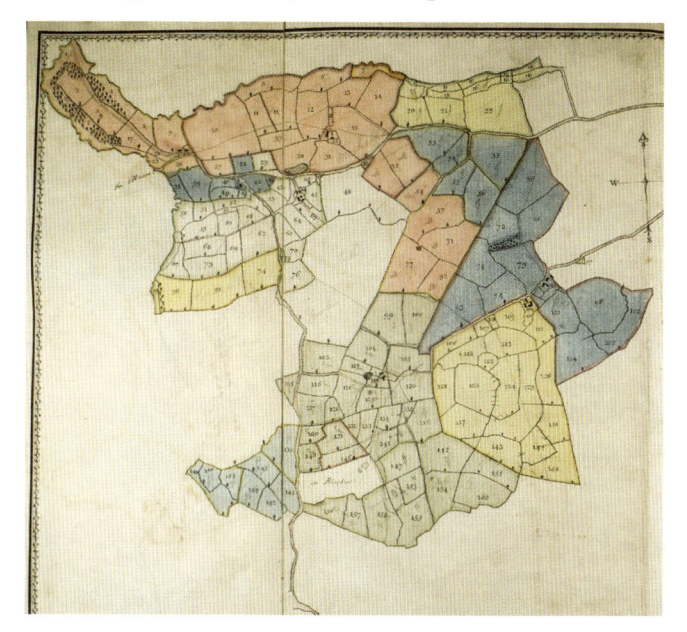

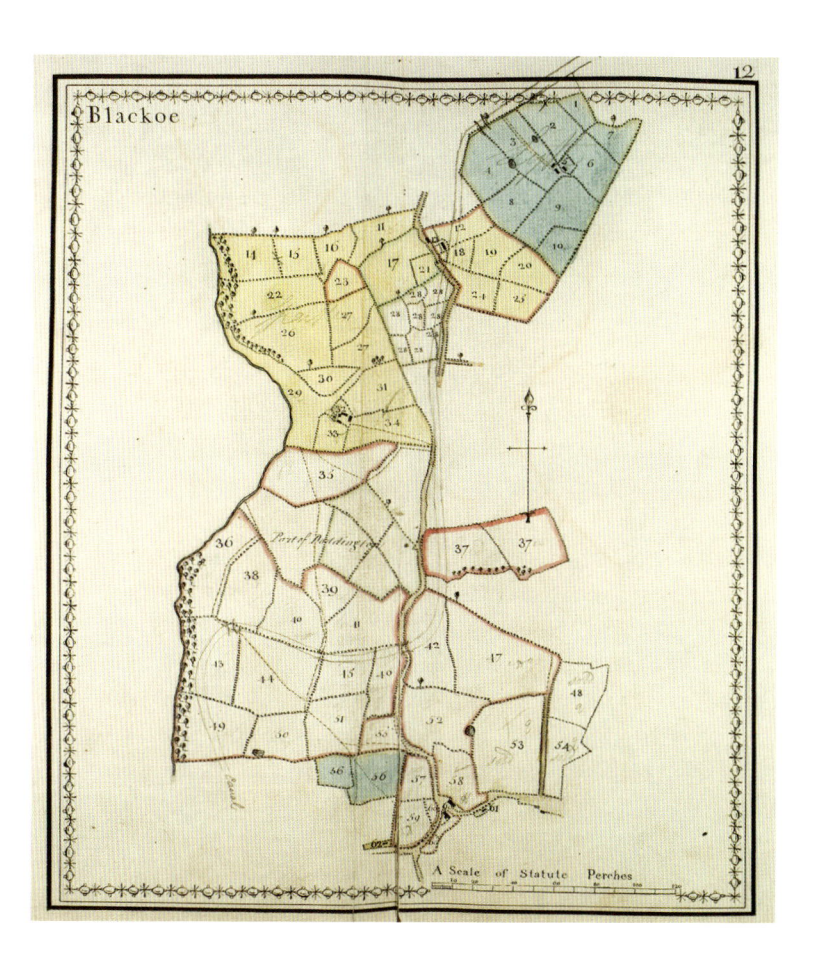

Above : *Blackoe as mapped by George Grey 1761 in a tightly bound book. Most of the plans cross the spine to cover two pages.*

Left : *Dodington in the Book of Maps contrasts markedly with the same area shown on the large map of the whole manor.*

between surveys. Some farms were recognisably almost the same at both dates; some small territories of 1651 had been amalgamated when Grey plotted them. The Nevit family still had a butterfly shaped property on the eastern edge in 1761; much of the land held by Thomas Burrowes in 1651 passed to Mr Dodd before 1761. William Spark, however, in 1761 had a farm which had been split between at least seven tenants in 1651, and J.Murhall in 1761 similarly occupied at least four of the 1651 farms, although he did not have them in a single block. George Barnes, incidentally, who may have been the blacksmith in the 1650s with a farm adjacent to the Nevit property, had been supplanted by T.Griffiths before 1761. He also held what had been Widow Bostock's land in 1651. The Roe family had appeared in Dodington by 1761 with Hugh Roe having a farm centred on that of Richard Hide and his neighbours John Lea and Richard Burrowes in 1651. A district split 32 ways in 1651 was divided among twenty people in 1761. As with Bubney, there is something unsatisfactory in the calculations of field areas as between Fowler and Grey for what looks to be the same space on the maps. Fowler had just over 750 acres for Grey's 641 or thereabouts.

If this pattern of fewer tenancies and larger properties could be traced in Black Park and Little Ash, for example, there might be a temptation to look for an estate bailiff or agent who pushed for this as a policy. Alexander Duncombe, who so acted in the earliest years of the eighteenth century, might fit the bill, but nothing can be proved at this stage. Nationally, it is well established that during the eighteenth century land moved out of the hands of many modestly endowed yeoman farmers into the possession of fewer tenants of expanded farms. Some of the greater aristocratic estates set the pace of change at a faster rate than others, but it remains to be seen where the Bridgewaters came in the race to maximise profits from land holdings. Whitchurch manor was but a small part of the family's interest.

Grey's survey

In the manor as a whole :-
169 separate individuals held 209 plots of land between them

Unallocated areas were given as :-
Whitchurch Heath	347 acres
Brown Moss	77 acres
Oss Mere	36 acres
Blakemere	17 acres
Steel Heath	1 acre
Wastes and lanes	143 acres

In addition, 9 plots had not been accounted for, plus 64 acres on which the town stood and a plot donated for Tilstock chapel, which made a total of 5913 acres by Grey's calculation.

End Notes

1. Hugh Malet *Bridgewater the Canal Duke 1736-1803* (1977)
2. ShropA 212/472
3. Hertfordshire County Record Office AH2770
4. P. Eden *Dictionary of Land Surveyors and Local Mapmakers of Great Britain and Ireland 1530-1850* (2nd edit 1997)
5. In the Book of Maps Grey included on his title page an intention to produce maps of the Duke's Lancaster properties, but carefully crossed out this reference for some unknown reason, see ShropA 212/479/3-4

1761 Map of farms and their occupiers in Dodington with Blackoe

This map has been compiled from George Grey's survey and schedule to show the field patterns of individual leasehold farms and their occupiers as he found them in 1761.

Name	acres
Bedward, G	11
Benson, J	17
Dodd, Mr	117
Griffiths, T	76
Liversage, T	23
Lyth, J	79
Lyth, T	40
Murhall, J	153
Nevit, J	80
Nevit, W	56
Ravenshaw, J	10
Roe, H	92
Spark, W	74
Turton, Mr	5
Watson, J	4
Deaves, C	17
Downes, A	12

Eight others not shown on map had less than 1 acre

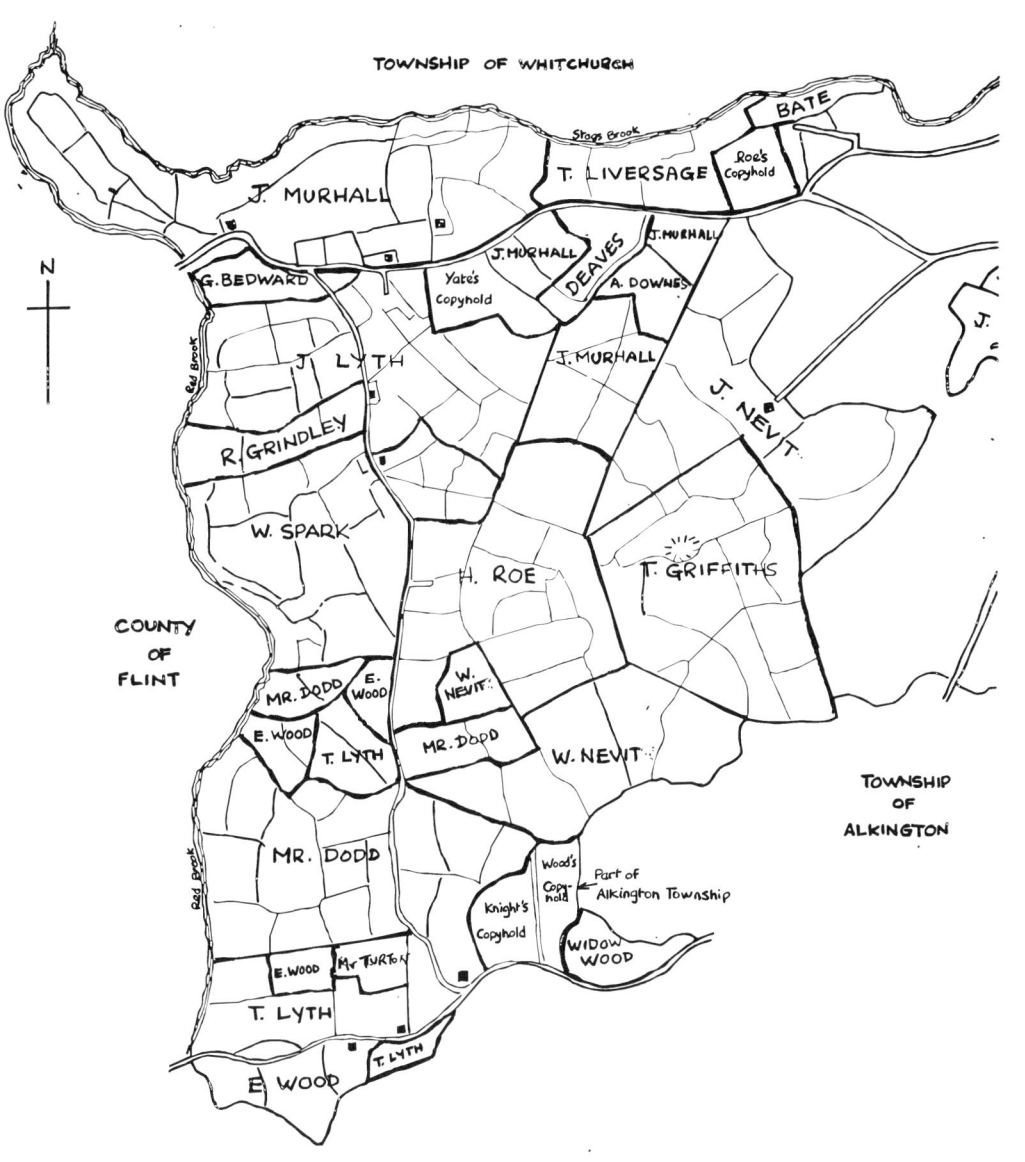

The view over Jubilee Park from Newtown car park

Whitchurch mills

The view from the car park overlooking the band stand in Whitchurch Park has its attractions, but it hardly reveals the historical importance of this stretch of land. Why is there a public park here? Whose jubilee is memorialised in its name: who established the park and when? Even more mystifying, what was here before the park was created? This is a pleasant view today, but how has it come to be like this?

Easy answers to some of these questions take us back, as already explained, to the Victorian age. It was Queen Victoria's Golden Jubilee in 1887 which was celebrated by raising money for the park. It was her Diamond Jubilee in 1897 which brought further development of this public space. Stated like this, it seems simple; but these spare facts hide controversy and anxieties in late Victorian Whitchurch from which the Park emerged.

Not that this is the start of the story, however. This was land with a long history before Victoria was even conceived, let alone came to the throne. The Park lies in a valley which defines the western boundary of the ancient settlement built over ruins of a Roman fort. There was a late Norman castle for a brief time looking across this exact same territory. A valley implies a stream – but none is obvious today. Proximity to a medieval urban community implies the possibility of open field farming around the congregation of dwellings. Was this valley and hillside beyond hay meadow or arable land? The questions are further complicated by local knowledge that a canal ran along this valley terminating in a wharf up against Mill

The view park over Jubilee Park towards New Street 2007

Street. This was an arm of the main Ellesmere- Chester canal (later known as the Shropshire Union) which initially by-passed the town a couple of miles to the west. A wharf at Grindley Brook was the commercial link with Whitchurch. This branch canal has clearly been filled in and removed from the landscape, leaving scarcely a trace at this end of its line. Who built this water-way, when and with what consequences? Just to add one other feature of this area, what about the previous use of the land on which the car park is situated?

Many different pieces of evidence allow these questions to be answered. One source of clues to the history of this Jubilee Park area lies in a series of sketch plans stored away in the collections of the Bridgewater family, lords of Whitchurch manor. They point to the importance of a water-course flowing through the town and away westward to the Red Brook and the River Dee. In particular, they reveal how Whitchurch depended for power on this stream called Stags Brook. Water driven corn mills were essential features of the economies of English towns and villages throughout the medieval period, and into the early nineteenth century at least. Whitchurch mills lay alongside and across a stream which wound its way around the town from Blakemere in the east to Bubney Moor and Iscoyd Park in the west. Rights to use the flow of the stream and the water itself had financial value to those with adjacent land, as well as to the lord of the manor. As is often the case, the historian benefits from documents left behind from disputes about rights, or from papers drawn up for some development which never took place.

The earliest sketch plan cannot easily be dated, but has been ascribed to 1598. The basis for this is some notes written over part of one of the two sheets which together make the plan.[1] It is a simple outline of a series of pools along a water-course leaving Blakemere and passing through *'Park Pole, Way Mill Pole, Town Pole, Sherye Mill Pole, Olde Newe Mill pole, Newe Mill Pole, The mill to be made'*. These are familiar places today.

The date is significant as the time when Whitchurch was sold to the Egerton family, later Earls and Dukes of Bridgewater. It is entirely possible that Sir Thomas Egerton wanted a plan of the stream and mills over which he exercised his lordship. On the other hand, this plan may be the work of Christopher Saxton, the leading map-maker of this period. A survey of the Whitchurch estate in 1597 by Henry Caldcote is said to have been done with the assistance of Saxton. If this was the case, the sketch plan was for Edward Talbot shortly before selling the estate.[2]

On the plan seven mill buildings are shown with associated pools. Six of the mills are sketched with one wheel each, but at the mill west of *Newe mill pole* three wheels are shown. The naming of this building indicates that it was not only the pool which had been created but that an additional mill had been erected also. What had once been a New Mill had been succeeded by another, and hence the first had been renamed the Old New Mill. A note on the plan, detailing leases and rents, appears to state that one or other of the New Mills was a specialised malt mill. In Caldcote's survey, however, only five mills were noted each paying separate rents though three of them were leased to John Bolland. By 1600 Bolland only had Shirrey Mill, while Town Mill, Park Mill and New Mill were held by Roger Brereton. Way Mill was occupied by John Gill.[3] There was, incidentally, a decayed windmill in the manor according to the same survey.

This plan of the water-course through Whitchurch in late Elizabethan times not only shows two more mills than the 1598 Survey listed, but has one of them noted as *'The mill to be made'*. It's a nice question as to whether or not there is evidence here of some period of prosperity and economic expansion which had been enjoyed rather earlier than the 1590s requiring an increase in milling capacity. If so it was followed by one of the New Mills being left unoccupied. The map is evidence that there were plans to erect a seventh mill further west still, which rather suggests that there had been recovery from economic slump. The

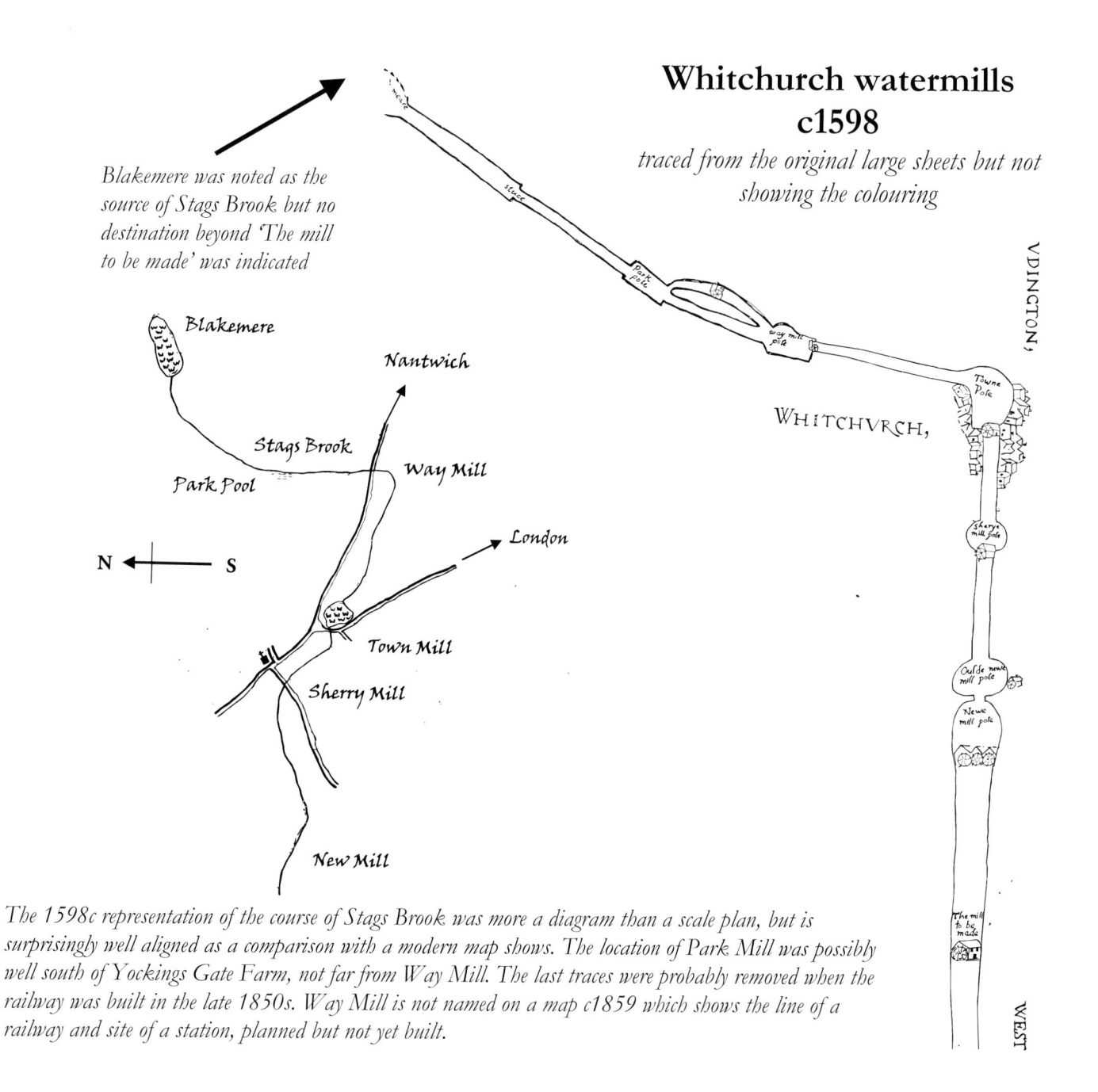

Whitchurch watermills c1598

traced from the original large sheets but not showing the colouring

Blakemere was noted as the source of Stags Brook but no destination beyond 'The mill to be made' was indicated

The 1598c representation of the course of Stags Brook was more a diagram than a scale plan, but is surprisingly well aligned as a comparison with a modern map shows. The location of Park Mill was possibly well south of Yockings Gate Farm, not far from Way Mill. The last traces were probably removed when the railway was built in the late 1850s. Way Mill is not named on a map c1859 which shows the line of a railway and site of a station, planned but not yet built.

puzzle is that no later evidence has been found to show that it was, in fact, built.

What does seem clear is that the period when more milling power was necessary came before the 1370s. A New Mill already existed at that time in addition to Town Mill, Sherry Mill and Upper and Middle Mills. [4] If this was the Old New Mill then a sixth mill was constructed at some as yet unknown date. It is also a puzzle as to exactly where this second New Mill was located, and what its relationship was to the mill known by this name and which survived into the eighteenth century. Way Mills, incidentally, probably called Middle Mills at first, stood at a point where 'the way' or road to Nantwich crossed Stags Brook. This was clearly marked by John Roque on his map of Shropshire in 1752. [5]

In 1761 Grey plotted three mills on his maps. Town Mill appeared on his street plan of the town, and Way Mill and New Mill were shown on his plan of Whitchurch township. The only other pool which Grey noted had no name but was in the stretch of land between the Town Mill and the point where Sherry Mill Road crossed Stags Brook – in other words, in what is now Jubilee Park, immediately below the car park in Newtown. This pool was the subject of a plan drawn in 1739 almost certainly as a consequence of some dispute about rights to the use of the stream. This time it was not a corn mill which was at issue, but a waterworks.

The disappearance of Sherra or Sherry Mill cannot be dated, nor can the end of Park Mill be fixed. Neither of them appeared on the 1752 map by Roque. In the early eighteenth century, however, there was a scheme by which water was pumped up to Newtown almost certainly to flow into pipes for delivery to houses in High Street. In 1739 the waterworks was closely defined on a plan drawn for the Duke of Bridgewater to clarify the rights of property holders in the neighbourhood. [6]

This operation required a pool named on the plan as Payne's Pool and dug out 'within 3 years last past'. Water from the pool powered a wheel in turn driving a pump or 'engine' raising water up the slope for use in the town. Payne enjoyed the rights over a water supply only so long as the lord of the manor agreed – 'at will' as the phrase was. One interesting feature was that Stags Brook was not the source for water taken up to houses. Instead, this came from a spring across the narrow valley in Scotland Fields. What Payne supplied, in other words, was fresh drinking water, an indication surely that this commodity was insufficiently available from wells. Perhaps here is also a sign of some prosperity and social aspiration among the traders and artisans in Whitchurch.

Richard Payne was himself described as a gentleman in the Memorandum accompanying the plan and was probably not the entrepreneur who managed the water works directly. Indeed, he may not have been the initiator of the project for in 1722 Gabriel Nicholls and Jonathan Taylor were named in manor court records as the proprietors 'of the waterworks in Whitchurch'. They were complaining at the time about the behaviour of a butcher, Robert Barrow the younger, who had allowed his garden to collapse into the brook thus stopping up and slowing down the flow of water they needed to drive their wheel. [7] It is entirely possible that it was the frequency of this kind of action which forced Payne in his capacity of landlord, or waterworks operator, to dig out a proper mill pool to guarantee a free flow of water to drive the pump.

Another plan dated three years later provides more

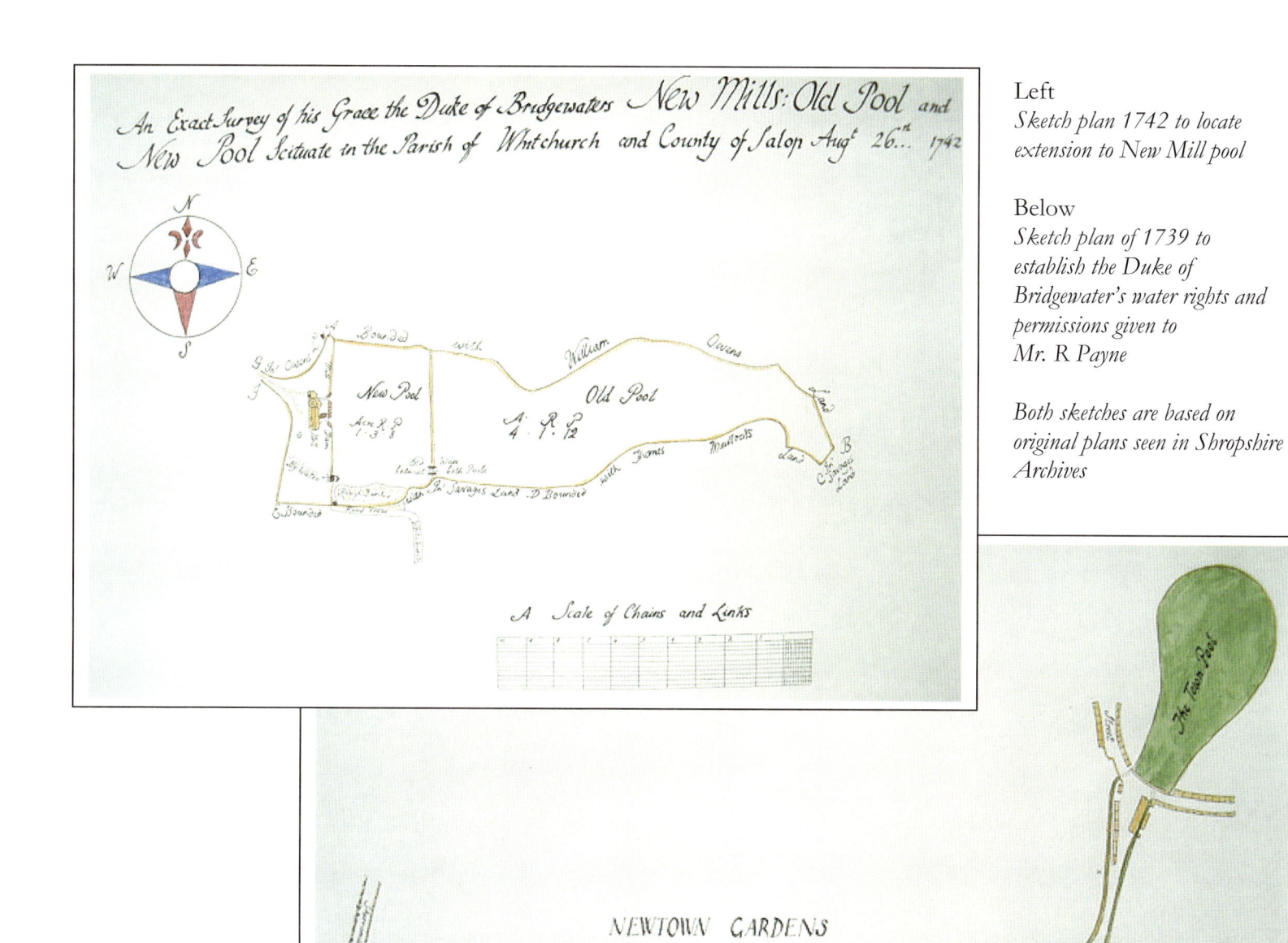

Left
Sketch plan 1742 to locate extension to New Mill pool

Below
Sketch plan of 1739 to establish the Duke of Bridgewater's water rights and permissions given to Mr. R Payne

Both sketches are based on original plans seen in Shropshire Archives

information about New Mills.[8] In 1742 an extension to the pool was intended – perhaps carried out – at the mill furthest west along Stags Brook, a site Grey included on his 1761 map. The proposal was to enlarge the area under water by bringing it close up to the mill building, presumably doing away with a leet from the old pool. This mill came into the possession of the Jebb family as tenants on the Bridgewater estate from at least 1778.

There is more to be discovered about Park Mill and its disappearance and when Sherry Mill ceased to be water driven. Town Mill was taken down when the canal was constructed to a wharf in Mill Street. In effect, it was replaced by the Lord Hill Hotel about 1810. The history of Way Mill is incomplete, but the New Mill story is continued as part of the history of Chemistry. Finally, the stretch of Stags Brook from Watergate and the Lord Hill Hotel to Chemistry becomes part of the history of the canal and the development of Jubilee Park. Ultimately, the stream was culverted and the canal filled in to produce the landscape as seen today from Newtown car park.

End Notes

1. ShropA 212/413
2. Mary C. Hill, *Shropshire Records: a guide to the County Record Office stock* (1952) p90. Edward Talbot, lord of Whitchurch, was the younger brother of the Earl of Shrewsbury.
3. Hopkins thesis p147-8. Roger Brereton was an esquire in the 1600 Rental for the estate, holding New Mills for £20 per year – hence he was not the miller! ShropA 212/97. Bolland was also known as Bowland see 212/413 notes on map.
4. Francesca B.G.Bumpus *Society, government and power in the Lordship of Blakemere, North Shropshire c1350 – 1420* Univ Coll of Wales, Aberystwyth, unpublished PhD 1998 p47 and 166
5. Way Mill was possibly known at first as Middle Mill and appears in the accounts of Blakemere 1419-20 under this name see Barbara Ross, *Accounts of the Stewards of the Talbot Household at Blakemere 1392-1425* (2003) p137. It had been built before 1387, Francesca B.G.Bumpus *Society, government and power in the Lordship of Blakemere, North Shropshire c1350 – 1420* Univ Coll Wales, Aberystwyth unpublished PhD 1998 p47
6. ShropA 212/413
7. Whitchurch Manor Court Presentments 2 April 1722 ShropA 212/Box 48, but works there by 1718 see ShropA 212/Box 47
8. ShropA 212/413

Black Park farms 1761-1839 and a field survey 1814

Some explorations into Whitchurch history can't be guided by ready-made maps – at least, not ones that are convenient. In fact, a purpose for carrying out an investigation can be to compile a new map based on evidence only available as text – or to make comparisons with maps of other dates. This is the case for Black Park in 1814.

Sketch plans of individual farms, with every field named, were drawn in a notebook started in 1814 as part of a wider survey of the Bridgewater estate. The intention was to record how each piece of ground was used. [1] These sketches can be plotted on to a district map and then compared with the earlier survey conducted by George Grey in 1761, as well as a later map constructed for the Tithe Commissioners in the late 1830s. [2] Black Park was always the most desirable section of Whitchurch manor and those who had leases there counted at all times as among the principal inhabitants of the neighbourhood.

The notebook doesn't contain the name of the person who proposed a systematic register of land use, but the plan was to enter information about crops each year at least until 1822. It was probably made by the agent for the seventh Earl of Bridgewater as a working document to keep track of what tenants on the estate were doing. In some cases, data was duly entered, but not completely for every farm in every year. There were numerous amendments and crossings out at various points which are assumed to indicate alterations noted as years passed by. A full statement was made, including field sizes, for 1814 which was the base line for the whole record and thus what is copied on to the present map. Eight principal tenants then worked Black Park with just over 1,300 acres between them.

Districts of the estate named in the notebook were Whitchurch, Black Park, Dodington, Bubney and Blackoe and an index of names referred to 28 people. It is not certain that all the farms across the estate, or all the tenants, were included in these lists. Outside Black Park tenants were recorded in much less detail with the exception of William Sparkes and Thomas Hughes in Blackoe, Thomas Lyth, whose farm lay south of the road to Ellesmere, Richard Murhall, and widows Roe and Price. In view of the doubts, and the omission of the two Ashes and both Woodhouses, the new map which incorporates sketches found in the notebook has been confined to Black Park.

The 1814 map of Black Park

The number in each field on the original sketches refers to a schedule of field names, with sizes noted in acres, rods and perches. The new map is based upon the field pattern as delineated by Grey in 1761 and checked against the tithe map of 1839. Field names are not consistent across the three sources, but there is sufficient coincidence of field shapes and names to be confident that the farm boundaries defined for 1814 are reasonably accurate. Eight major farms dominate the district, though an area on the western edge divided into several smallholdings fringed the urban settlement. They were not plotted out for purposes of the land use survey and cannot easily be associated with the name of a tenant. Their size varied up to just over seven acres and taken together they would have constituted a ninth important farm.

The pattern of farms and the names of tenants in 1814 have more meaning when comparisons are made with earlier and later evidence. The predominance of concentrated holdings is quite clear, with only Richard Williams and his successor, John Bradbury, having to deal with widely separated fields, although how far George Bradshaw was handicapped by Ossmere is a moot point.[3]

The map also poses rather than answers the question as to the value to the farming economy of both Ossmere and Blakemere, given that five of the eight tenants had access to the waters. Their rights over fishing, fowling and drainage would have been spelled out in leases not studied for present purposes. Incidentally, it is worth noting that any or all of the tenants could have farmed land outside this district, and in some other estate, so this map may not show the full extent of any one tenant's interests.

What shows up in comparison with 1761 is that several smaller tenancies had been consolidated by 1814 to give the Tudmans and William France substantial farms. The rate of reduction in numbers of leases on this part of the estate was still very slow and a question arises as to whether some kind of optimum size had been reached in relation to the available technologies of arable working and cattle management. The basic pattern of land division had not altered a great deal either, especially in the eastern half of the district where the largest properties lay.

Another clue to the relative stability of holdings from well before 1761 probably, and after 1839 certainly, is the fact there were only seven farmsteads built in the district.

Names of successive occupiers of farmsteads 1761, 1814, 1841
- J. Fallows, Thomas Prince, Thomas Maddocks
- E. Payne, Tudman, Arthur Dicken,
- J. Gibbons, William France, William France
- W. Bulkeley, William Sandford, John Sandford
- B. Blackmore, John Sandford junr, Thomas Hassall
- S. Sandford, John Sandford senr, William Redrop
- John Bradshaw, George Bradshaw, John Bradshaw
  ie Deaves and Bradbury had farmstead outside the district

Family histories for the Sandfords, Bradshaws and Princes would add greatly to the meaning of this map. Only the Sandfords and Bradshaws held properties at all three dates, with the Bradshaw family alone remaining attached to one stretch of ground. This does not argue for the conventional view that farming families, by and large, stayed put over many generations and rural populations were stable entities. An examination of the parish rate book for Whitchurch in 1794 adds detail to the story, but does not alter the general conclusion. For example, neither the Bradburys nor their predecessors, the Williams family, were present in 1794, but one had replaced the other by 1814.

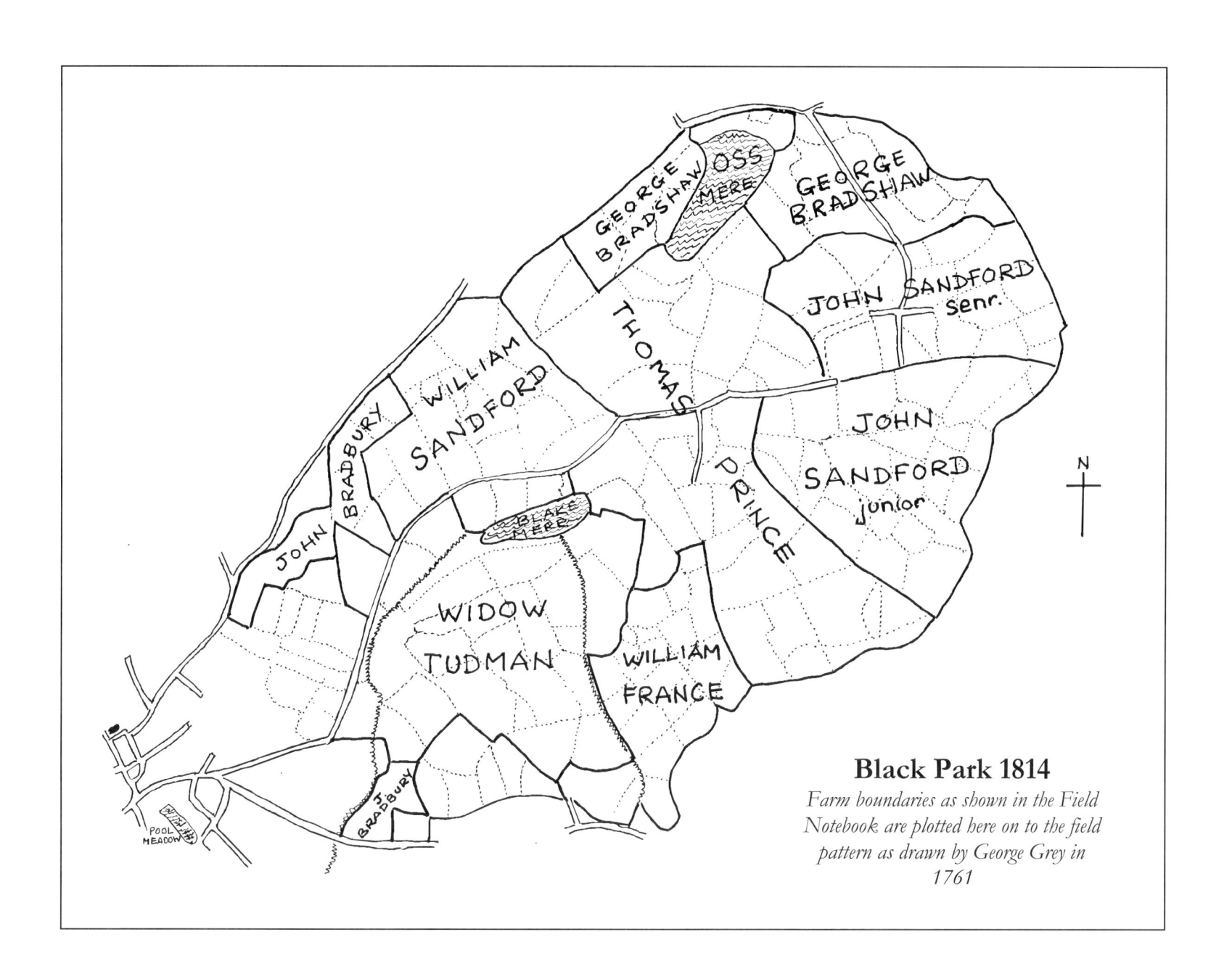

Black Park 1814

Farm boundaries as shown in the Field Notebook are plotted here on to the field pattern as drawn by George Grey in 1761

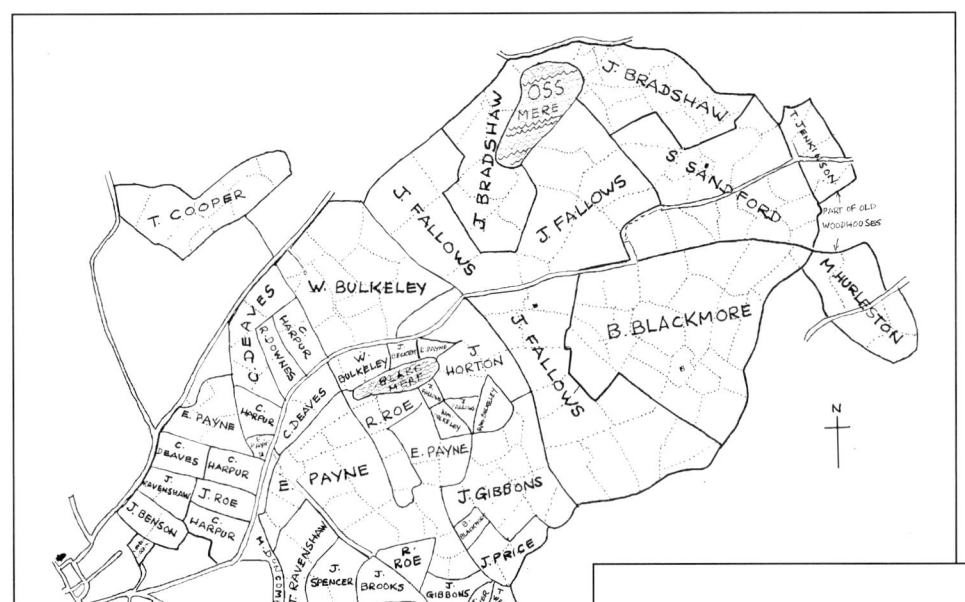

Above : **Black Park 1761**
George Grey's survey for the Duke of Bridgewater with the principal tenants named

Right : **Black Park 1839**
Survey for the Tithe Commissioners with the names of the principal tenants inserted

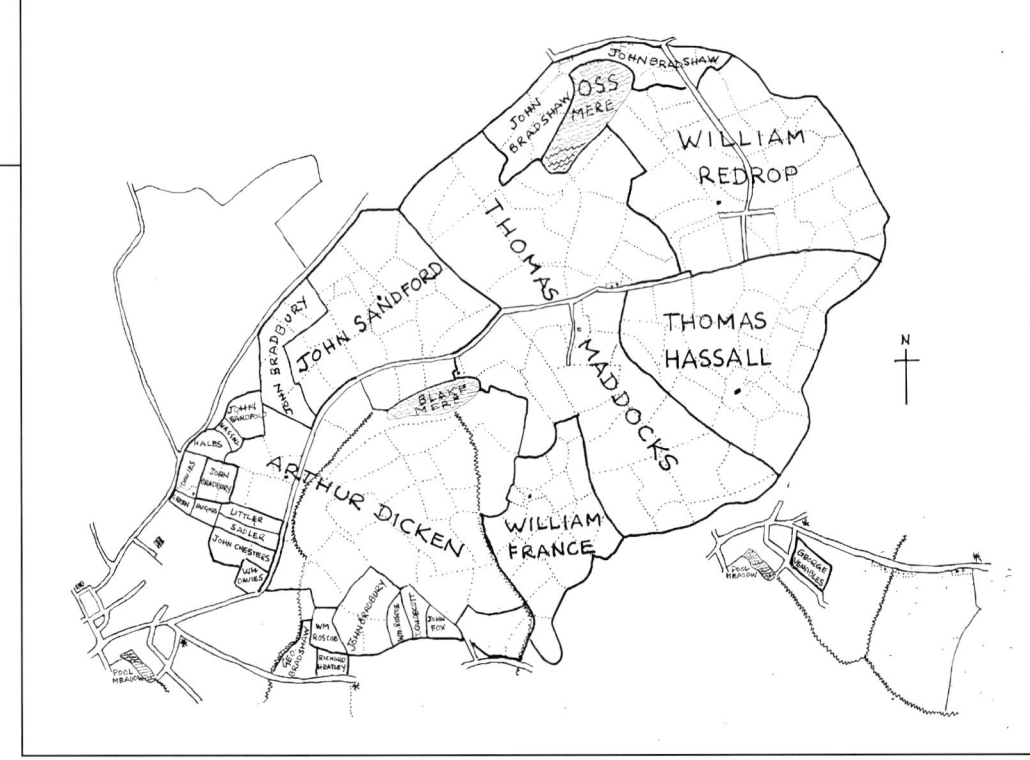

Land use

The distinctive feature of the notebooks is the recording of how each field was used. This snapshot of farming is of great interest despite covering only a part of Whitchurch and with data confined to 1814. There were probably also special conditions applicable to that year influencing the balance between arable and pasture.

The first of the Tables shows the chief statistics, and the proportion of land used for cereals is a point worth stressing. Assuming that land left fallow for the year was in the arable rotation, some 43% was plough land, and virtually 25% had cereals growing that year. The evidence supplied in the notebooks does not suggest whether these were typical percentages or unusual ones. North Shropshire in general would be considered dairy country and such an amount of cereal growing could be unexpectedly high. If this were the case, it would be important to recall that there was still a major European war affecting the level of corn imports. High prices for the staples of bread and beer-making encouraged farmers to plough up grassland to supply a demanding market. There was, however, much concern that these favourable conditions would change immediately on peace being restored. In fact, in 1815 Parliament enacted notorious legislation to protect British farmers from vast quantities of cheaper grain imports – the Corn Laws bedevilled politics for the next thirty years and more.

Grassland was not necessarily permanent pasture, and cattle were not the only animals kept. However, a quick study of the partial set of figures for these farms for the years after 1814 suggests that much of the 53% of land down to grass was permanently so used. Few fields noted as having grass were ever ploughed

BLACK PARK: Land use in acres Name of tenant 1814	Oats	Clover	Wheat	Fallow	Barley	Grass	Total acreage
Prince, Thomas	50	26	32	35	8	176	327
Tudman, Widow (possibly widow of Robert according to index) *	17	23	79	22	0	97	238
Sandford, William	0	11	19	9	8	85	132
Sandford, John senr	15	19	17	18	0	81	150
Sandford, John, jnr	12	10	29	17	0	107	175
Bradshaw, George	11	10	9	13	0	80	123
Bradbury, John (formerly Richard or Robert Williams)	0	0	7	0	6	55	68
France, William *	0	11	6	11	0	70	98
Total of above	105	110	198	125	22	751	1311
					42.7%	57.2%	

Italics indicates that the same Christian name and surname appeared in the 1794 Rate Book as a Bridgewater tenant
* indicates the same surname in the 1794 Rate Book as a Bridgewater tenant
Rods and perches have been ignored in acreage measurements

within the cereal-fallow-clover rotation. Evidently, this was cattle country.

The other sparse statistics available for 1814 in the Notebooks reinforce this conclusion. William Sparkes, Thomas Lythe, Richard Murhall and Widow Roe collectively had 72% down to grass and only 14% planted with oats and wheat. None of them had barley – in fact, there was only a little grown in Black Park. These four worked approximately 600 acres between them, leaving two obviously large farms with useful maps in the notebook, but unaccounted for. There was no land use information recorded for either Thomas Hughes or Widow Price – a gap of well over 400 of the 2,300 or so acres otherwise subject to scrutiny by the Earl of Bridgewater's agent.

One conclusion possible from this notebook is that by 1814 the Bridgewater interest in the area for revenue purposes had shrunk a good deal. A short list was appended of tenants each of whom held little more than a cottage, sometimes with a garden, or a small field. Locations weren't plotted, but field names were noted. Thomas Wood had the Higher and Lower Shooting Butts – just over ten acres in all – Joseph Beckett had part of the Great Field. Richard Pearce was among the few who had houses. A link with the feudal past was William Cook's lease of the tolls of Whitchurch – presumably on market stalls – while the Bridgewaters' more recent interest in canals was demonstrated by Naylor, Hassall & Co renting the wharf at the terminus of the canal arm linking the town to the wider world down the waterway now known as the Shropshire Union canal.

1794 Parish Rate Book : Black Park

List of tenants on the Bridgewater estate and area of land leased in acres, rods and perches

	A	R	P
Bradshaw, George	123	2	33
Court, Ann	15	3	0
Crosse, Ann	22	3	34
Deaves, Richard	25	3	36
Downes, John	1	2	24
Downs, John	11	1	26
Egerton, F H	53	3	15
France, Mary	76	3	20
Hughes, John	8	2	23
Morris, George	11	3	11
Price, Mary	15	3	36
Prince, Thomas	321	1	23
Sandford, John	132	2	24
Sandford, William	180	0	38
Tagg, William	13	0	12
Tomkin, Richard	141	1	33
Tudman, Robert	123	3	3
Tudman, Robert, late Cooper	23	1	9
Weaver, Ann	8	1	2

Highlights show tenants with land elsewhere in parish

End Notes

1. ShropA 212/360
2. H.D.G. Foxall *Tithe Maps for Field Names* (1978) has been used as a guide to field names, ShropA C.68.7
3. Boathouse Field lay between the two halves of George Bradshaw's farm and was not in his holding.

Whitchurch about 1840 : explorations using Tithe Award maps

Maps made for the Tithe Commissioners are specially exciting for the Whitchurch historian. They were drawn between 1837 and 1842, but conventionally dated here to 1839. The Commissioners conducted a national inquiry according to the Tithe Commutation Act 1836. This laid down that traditional 'tithe' payments to Anglican clergy from their parishioners were to be standardised and translated into a money rent or charge on land. A fair assessment of this rent from all land holdings subject to tithe required lists of landholders and occupiers, and exact measurements of field size and estimates of soil quality.

Shropshire had an overwhelming proportion of its land subject to tithe, in contrast with some areas where enclosure by statute included commuting tithe payments. Whitchurch parish was almost entirely titheable. Field maps were drawn to plot the details of an Apportionment Award, or schedule, registering all the landowners, their tenants and the fields held by each tenant, together with acreages and land use. All this information was gathered before any Ordnance Survey mapmakers toured the area, and the only previous plans of the parish with which a comparison can be made were the estate plans drawn up for the Duke of Bridgewater in 1761 by George Grey – unfortunately, not an exactly like-for-like comparison.

One copy of the Whitchurch maps and Award was deposited in the diocesan archive and is now found at Lichfield. However, the correspondence between parish officials, locally-based surveyors and agents for the Commission, who visited the parish to hold meetings with residents and landowners, can be found in The National Archives at Kew, in the Tithe Files.[1] Here may be found any evidence of faults in the process, disputes and general information not registered in the schedule or on a map.

Whitchurch parish was mapped in fourteen sections and signed off as 'corrected and copied' by Bates and Timmis of Whitchurch. They are best examined township by township. Whitchurch (see map page 42) not only included a large section of the urban settlement, but also Bubney in the west and Black Park in the east. The photograph below is from the parish copy of this township's map, unfortunately cracked along a fold. The field numbers were registered in the accompanying Award. Unnumbered areas were sections of urban properties not subject to tithe.

A quick example of what can be discovered is found by looking at the north-west side of Claypit Street. Here, the crofts in a row numbered 337, 338, 339 and 340 were occupied by Rev. Charles Maitland Long (337 & 338 being 4 acres in extent) and George Harper esq., who held numbers 339 and 340 at 5 acres altogether. Maitland was a tenant of the Countess of Bridgewater, but Harper was an owner-occupier. There were no dwellings on their land in this stretch of the street, but on the opposite side of the

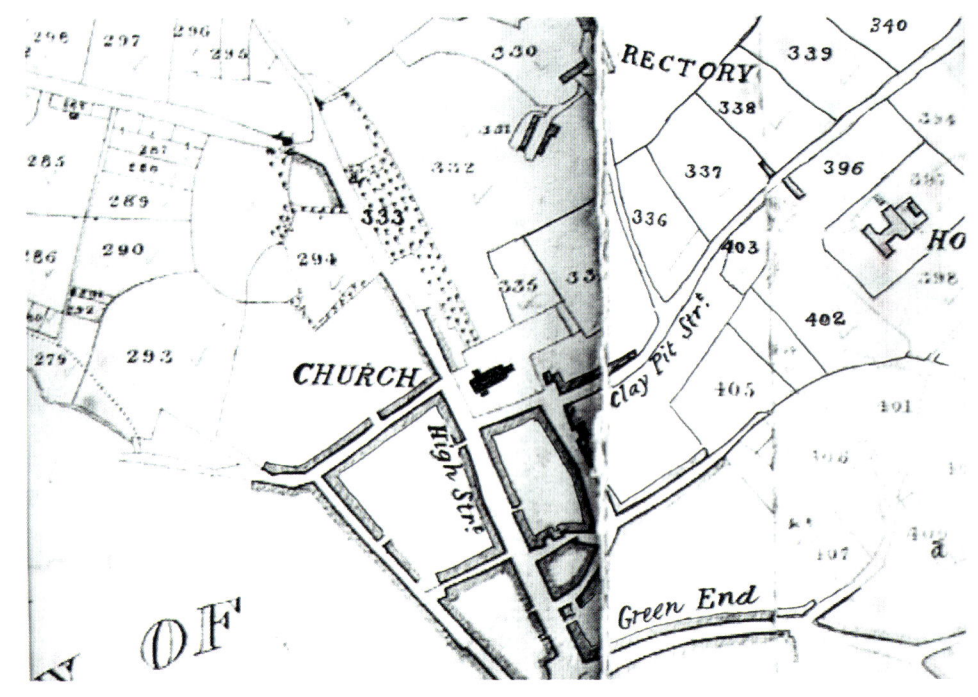

Left: *A damaged original Tithe map showing crofts on Clay Pit Street*

Below left: *Dodington farms and their occupiers adapted from the Tithe Award map 1839*

Below right: *Bubney farms and their occupiers taken from the Tithe map and Award 1839*

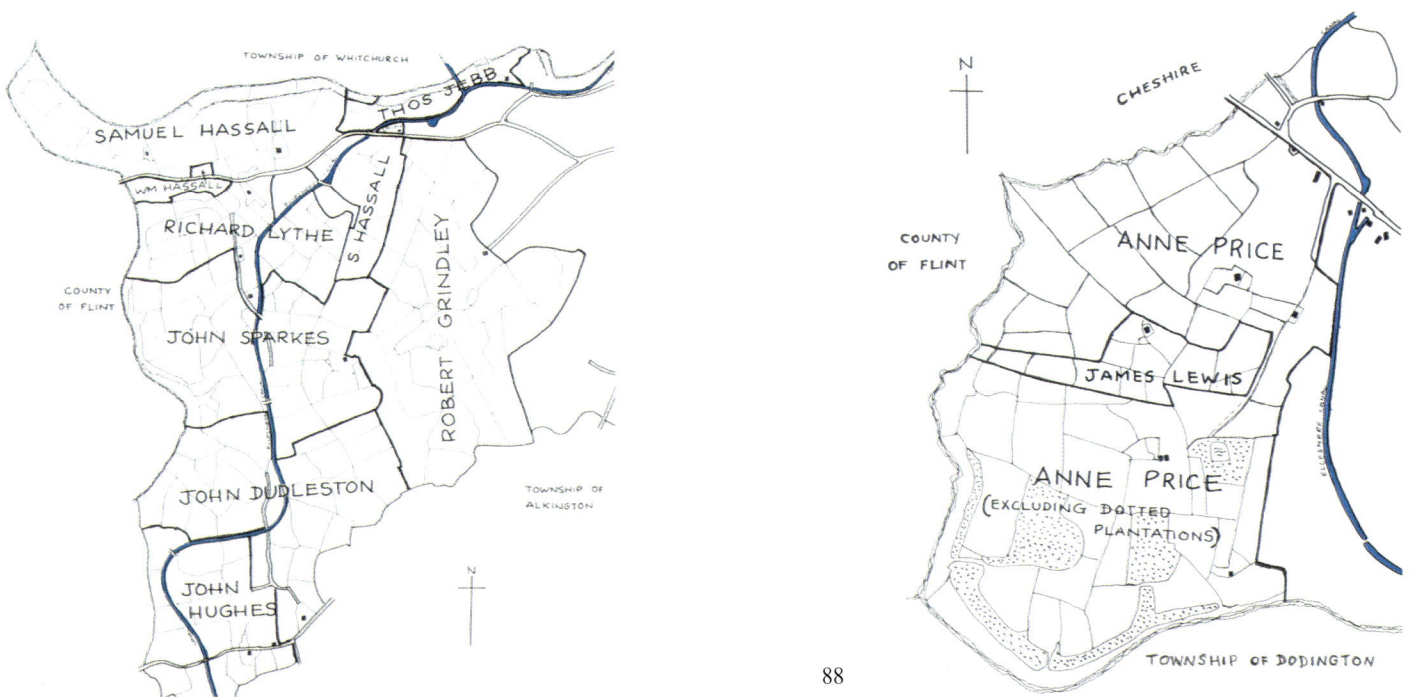

trackway was the House of Industry – Workhouse after 1834. Black Park farms as identified in the Tithe Award are plotted on the map on page 84 and farms in Bubney are shown on the page opposite to this.

Bubney shows a change from the situation in 1761 (see map page 70). Grey then found the district divided between three members of the Roe family, Arthur, Richard and John, with a fourth farm in the hands of Thomas Bickley. By 1837-42 Anne Price held all the property of the former Roe family (337 acres in all) and James Lewis had the only other property (33 acres). Woodland areas were retained as holdings of the Countess separate from the leases she made to Price and Lewis.

In Whitchurch township as a whole there were some 3,250 acres, of which the Countess of Bridgewater owned about 2,327 acres (72%). W.H.C.Poole was the only other owner with more than 100 acres in this township, but Robert Roe and the trustees for the late Robert Roe (presumably father and son) had an interest in about 155 acres. Robert had seven plots in his own right and shared ownership of three others with Robert Grindley Powell. The trustees owned eight plots the largest being nine acres leased to William Higgins. Philip Hales rented the bulk of this land (91 acres) from Robert Roe and his partner R.G.Powell.

Tenancies in Bubney about 1840 can be compared also with the pattern of landholding in 1651 (see page 47), and the same can be said for Dodington (see opposite) – or at any rate, that part of Dodington mapped by William Fowler (see page 48). Not the least of the changes since Grey's time in the landscape in this part of the Red Brook valley had been the construction of a canal. No doubt this severely affected the viability of farming small units. There could be other reasons, of course, but by the late 1830s

the ten separate plots surveyed by Grey had been reduced to five nucleated farms. Fowler had found twelve individual holdings in the same territory. Over the two centuries covered by the maps there was no continuity of family names. Only the Dodd family appeared on both the 1651 and 1761 maps, and only the Lythe, Sparkes and Grindley families were common to 1761 and the tithe map. It would appear that on the Bridgewater estate faming families did not continue much beyond a third generation, and then they were few and far between.

A pattern of landholding

A distinctive feature of the Whitchurch tithe maps is that they show who owned and occupied land outside the Bridgewater estate. This is not to say that it had always been independently owned, but that it was no longer counted as belonging to the Egerton family by the late 1830s. Just one small example of the distribution of properties demonstrates the richness of information contained in the tithe maps.

Whitchurch township contained the principal settlement of the ancient manor. In 1837 the lord of the manor was the widow of the seventh earl, Charlotte Catherine Anne, Countess of Bridgewater (1763-1849).[2] The surviving maps of her family's estate do not plot the boundaries of copyhold dwellings and crofts which were occupied by residents of the town – nor list those people by name. The great value of the maps done for the Tithe Commissioners in the late 1830s is that every field had to be mapped and identified as owned and occupied by particular persons.[3] This revealed the pattern of properties theoretically copyhold, but in practice owned by individuals. In other words, by comparing the ownership pattern across the

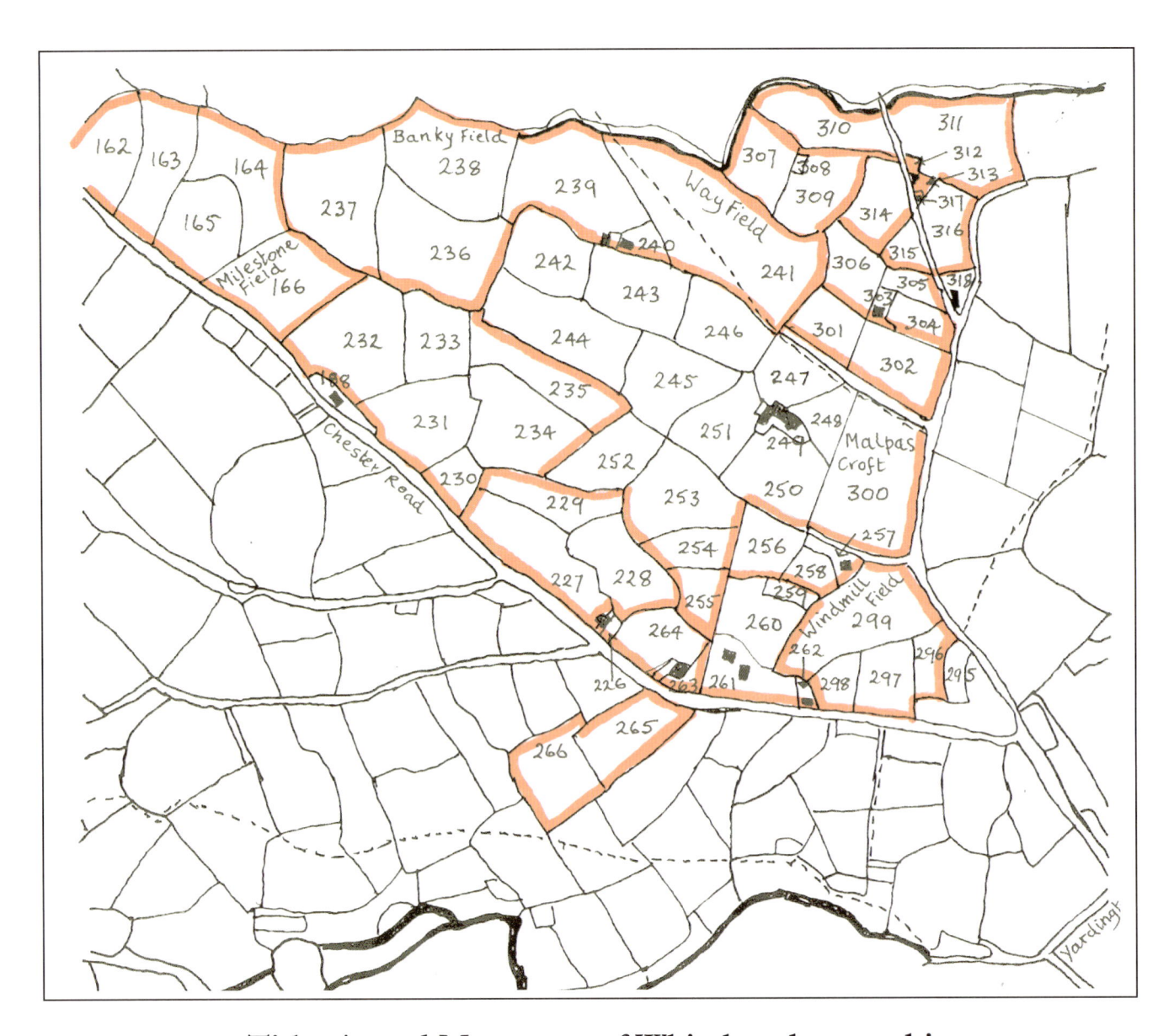

Tithe Award Map : part of Whitchurch township

This identifies individual properties as listed in Table A (opposite). Although the map is dated January 1842 the information refers back to the Award of December 1837 and the surveying must have been done between these dates.

1650, 1761 and 1830s maps it is possible to deduce how extensive and subdivided copyhold property had been since the early seventeenth century, although separate holdings were only shown on the 1839 Award map.

Table A : Whitchurch township

Owner	Field Nos	occupier
Grindley, R P	162 – 166	In hand
Roe, Robert	226	Skidmore, James
Roe, Robert	227 – 229	Green, Charles
Corser, Martha	230 – 235	Jones. J & T
Minton, Samuel	236 – 241	Bradbury, J
Worthington, Samuel	242 – 253	In hand
Worthington, Samuel	254 – 255	Lowe, J
Worthington, Samuel	300	In hand
Dymock, E F	256 – 258	In hand
Countze, Maria	259 – 261	Lowe, J
Countze, Maria	262	Grisdale, W & Walker, J
Worthington, T	263 – 64	Clay, Rev R B
Bridgewater, Countess	265 – 66	Groom, T
Bridgewater, Countess	296	Corser, G
Bridgewater, Countess	297	Francis, Mary
Bridgewater, Countess	298	Ragg, J
Bridgewater, Countess	299	Jebb, T
Litler, W	301- 02	In hand
Elliot, J	304 – 06	Elliot, Thomas
Trustees Trustees for Kempster & Barlow children	307 – 09	Venables, G
Duff, S A	310 – 312	Venables, Samuel
Edwards, J	313 – 14	Gostage, Elizabeth
Lakin, W	315 – 16	In hand
Tarporley Road Commissioners	317	Boyd, Allen
Butler, W	318	In hand
Basnet, Philip	319 – 20	In hand

Sub-letting of holdings had always been possible but manorial maps did not necessarily distinguish between holders and occupiers. This was a difference specifically reported in the Tithe Award. The current investigation is designed to identify something of the pattern of *ownership* in the new sense of 1839 within the areas which had been held of the Egertons by manorial custom for two hundred and forty years.

The records of successive manorial courts throughout the period of the Egerton possession listed what were technically called 'Admissions and Surrenders'. These show that a thriving land market existed in which rights to copyhold property were regularly bought and sold. The last Duke in the second half of the eighteenth century deliberately converted (ie sold) many, if not all, such copyhold lands into separately owned properties, though some might have just slid into that category by the 1830s without any formal paper record. The maps made for the Tithe Award are historically of great significance because they are the first plotting of the whole pattern of land ownership as it stood at one moment in time.

Only one small area of Whitchurch township is examined here.[4] The complexity of the pattern is typical of the whole parish however. In this section farms were consolidated more than was sometimes the case, but none were large. Samuel Worthington had the largest acreage at 40 and he worked the farm himself, while Martha Corser, who had fields including Great Meadow (232), owned nineteen acres plus one acre at the end of Green End called Deer Moss Croft. Samuel Minton possessed 29 acres, two of his fields being called 'Banky' (238, 236). He leased these to John Bradbury.

Incidentally, Bradbury tenanted 56 acres from the

Countess of Bridgewater in Black Park having taken this lease before 1814. He was an innkeeper in High Street according to the 1841 Census, aged fifty, with three sons, all pig dealers. In fact, he was a pork butcher himself, and combined this trade with being landlord at the Coach and Horses. [5]

At the other end of the scale were small plots owned by Thomas Worthington, who had two acres leased to Rev. R.B. Clay (263-4); William Butler, a publican at Grindley Brook, who had less than one acre in the angle where two roads joined on which he had his house (318); and John Edwards who had plots 313 and 314 rented by Elizabeth Gostage being two acres divided into very unequal parts by the road to Tarporley. [6] They were almost alongside the Tollgate House which belonged to the Tarporley Road Commissioners and was occupied by Allen Boyd. Close by were three acres owned by John Elliott (plots 303-6) across which by 1880 the London and North Western Railway had built a track known as the Tattenhall and Whitchurch Branch. [7]

Some of the field names are decidedly intriguing. Windmill Field stands out as a possible former site for a corn mill; Far Clapgate Field (307) is a puzzle – 'gate' can mean path or roadway rather than a swinging bar to control access. Way Field close alongside has a path marked across which is a sufficient explanation for it being on a route out of the township of ancient date, but not overused. Perhaps the path had moved from the adjacent field. Milestone Field, on the main road to Chester, suggests a name given since the early eighteenth century when milestones became a requirement - or perhaps not until the road was turnpiked in mid-century. The frequency of 'meadow' (232, 253) as a name, together with the numerous small 'crofts' (256, 258, 304) could be an indication of an earlier large common grazing ground – one of the town's fields of feudal times perhaps – which became enclosed by encroachment, or mutual agreement, in a rather haphazard fashion. Pit Field (245), Brick Kiln Field (260) and Well Field (247) may be self-explanatory, as is Barn Field (239).

One reference on the original map is difficult to interpret.[8] The words 'Oxford Carriers' are written in capital letters across fields 236, 239 and 241 in Minton and Worthington territory. The same font was used for township names which is most confusing. Does it have some connection with the 'Way' of Way Field, or the barns in field 240? The obvious connotation is to companies of carts or trains of pack horses carrying goods and people to or from Oxford at some time still remembered in the 1830s. It is difficult to see a cart owners' collective, if such there had been, owning this land. Did the map-makers fail to understand some local term for this area and make a curious error? Who knows?

Houses in this area are few and scattered. William Butler's home has been mentioned; John Lowe esq. occupied The Cottage (261) as tenant of Maria Countze with a Pleasure Ground attached -- a small orchard or wooded enclosure probably. He also rented two fields from Samuel Worthington (254, 255). In the 1841 Census he was noted as a banker with an address in Bargates. Samuel Worthington had a substantial farmstead more or less in the middle of his property (249). By 1880 this was known as Mount Farm. Elizabeth Frances Dymock had a cottage (257) which had been redeveloped by 1880, as a substantial house called Casula is shown at this point on the 1880 edition of the Ordnance Survey map. Rev. Clay lived on his rented land just a few yards west of The Cottage on the Chester Road. Otherwise, the only other homes mentioned were two cottages rented from Maria

Countze by William Grisedale and Joseph Walker (262), a gardener, on the Chester Road east of The Cottage.

In fact, this part of Whitchurch township has not been extensively developed for housing. Even on maps surveyed 1964-74 there is very little building shown on the north side of Chester Road. The only housing estate lies on fields owned in 1837 by William Litler, a butcher in Claypit Street, and those of John Elliot abutting the line of a railway track which had come and gone between 1839 and 1964.[9]

The Countess of Bridgewater did hold two small properties in this part of Whitchurch – fields leased out to five tenants – but the predominant impression of the area is a patchwork of independently owned territories often sub-let. The urban settlement was virtually surrounded by a ring of such small-holdings, a condition which partially determined the extent and manner of the expansion of the town in the later nineteenth and twentieth centuries.

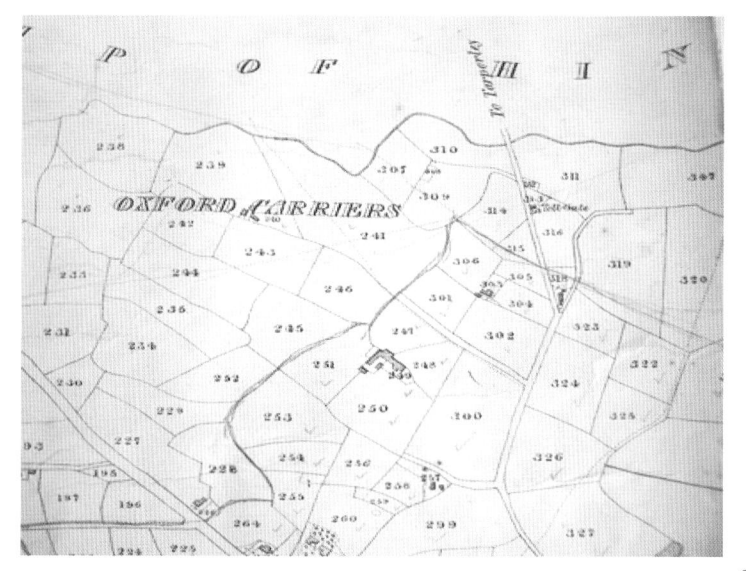

End Notes

1. Reference at The National Archives is IR18.
2. Charlotte, née Haynes, daughter of Colonel Samuel Haynes of Welbeck St, Marylebone at time of her marriage. Rights to Whitchurch manor were conveyed to her by her marriage settlement.
3. Town houses and gardens were not subject to tithe as this levy was, theoretically, one tenth of the annual produce of cultivated or pasture land and thus essentially on animal and human foodstuffs not on the profits of commerce or manufacture.
4. The basis for this map is the copy of the Tithe Award map kept in the church of St. Alkmund's cross-checked with H.D.G.Foxall *Tithe Maps for Field Names* (1978) ShropA C.68.7
5. See the 1814 Notebooks noted on page 82 for the earliest information about John Bradbury. Pigot's *Directory* 1835 lists him in these trades which he had followed for some time as well as being owner of a slaughter house and stable according to the Parish Rate Valuation in 1827. In 1849 a *Directory* lists him in Claypit Street as a pork butcher.
6. See 1841 Census for William Butler aged 63, and a Thomas Gostage, a butcher aged 40, in Castle Hill, Whitchurch.
7. See 1880 edition Ordnance Survey 25" to mile.
8. Foxall left this off his tracing of field boundaries.
9. For Litler see 1841 Census.

A photograph of part of the original tithe map

The heart of Whitchurch

Grey's plan 1761 (left) compared with the 1859 plan (right) shows developments over a century of change on the east side of High Street. The site of the Coach and Horses and 1872 Market and Town Hall was listed by Grey as two houses and a yard in High Street. The eighteenth century Town Hall is plainly marked on both map as a rectangle with dotss.

Whitchurch Market

From earliest days towns have thrived when their weekly markets flourished and Whitchurch is no exception. In Shropshire, at one time or another in the medieval period, there were at least 49 places where market trading was legally possible.[1] By the beginning of the seventeenth century one count found about eighteen still operating, Whitchurch included.[2] Friday markets gave Whitchurch an economic reason for existing second only to its location on a well-used route-way from Ireland and Chester through the Midlands to London.[3] In the longer term, its nearest commercial rivals, Prees and Malpas, lost out as did Audlem: on the other hand, Wrexham, Ellesmere, Wem and Market Drayton continued to have active markets.

In the history of Whitchurch a major theme giving continuity to accounts of change is that of retail trading. Perishable foods and hardware were of special importance as was the sale of live animals. The key form of trading, the earliest and longest lasting, was a legally controlled market. By definition, these weekly events were individually ephemeral and are easily overlooked because traders left few, if any, accounts of their activities. Buyers sometimes listed purchases and prices in their private estate household registers, and travellers made superficial judgements about prosperity. Necessarily, these references are scattered and difficult to trace. Records of those who policed market regulations rarely survive - very much the case for Whitchurch. Until the twentieth century, however, open markets were critical elements in the economy of Whitchurch and deserve fuller investigation.

Origins and early activity

The right to hold a market was, in effect, a stop on others setting up similar retail trading centres close by. Whitchurch was among the earliest places in Shropshire to get this local monopoly, obtained in a charter from Richard I in the 1190s. Shrewsbury, Oswestry and Bridgenorth were sites of markets so long before this that they did not require legal documentation, but Whitchurch was among the communities which claimed royal privilege. This, at least, was the burden of a case at Shropshire Assizes in 1292 when the manorial lord was required to prove the legality of the market and he showed a century old charter from Richard I as evidence. This is a document which has not been seen since, but the story at least indicates the likelihood that trading had gone on at a weekly market for more years than people could remember in 1292.[4]

Annual fairs were organised on the same legal basis. In 1362 Edward III issued a charter to John le Strange, lord of Whitchurch manor, allowing a fair to be held at the time of the festival of Simon and Jude the Apostles – that is 28 October.[5] This seems to be a second fair as a Whitsuntide fair had already been established.

The operation and development of the market must be assumed to be very similar to others elsewhere. Scattered evidence refers to 'shops' by the 1390s and a 'great hall'

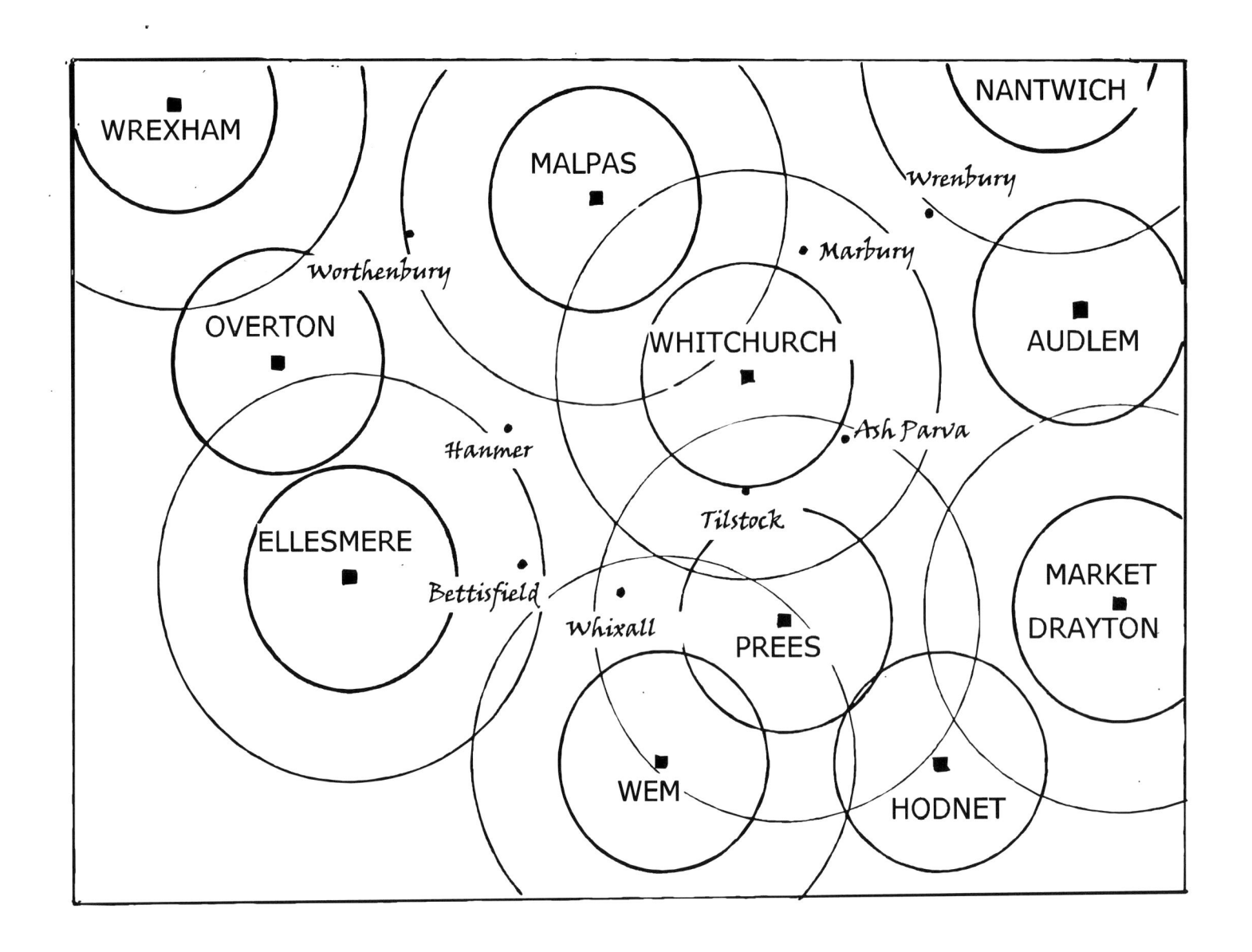

The distribution of medieval markets
Those recorded as active about 1516 are at the centre of circles of five miles radius, and if still open in approximately 1600 are with ten mile circles.

which implies the existence of some permanent retail premises as well as a covered space for market stalls.[6] In the 1590s there are references to rents for shops one of which is under the hall – presumed to be a communal building with a trading space on the ground floor. Had permanent shops been constructed on former open space originally for stalls?

Thomas Egerton was required in 1616 to prove his right to Whitchurch manor, markets, fairs and parks in answer to a royal *quo warranto* writ. He didn't leave a copy of a charter, but he obviously confirmed his rights.[7] In 1637 Richard Hyde, the Egerton's estate bailiff, built *'a little place in Whitchurch where poore people may sit in the dry and sell butter and cheese'*. Was this an addition to or a replacement for retail facilities?[8] In a manorial survey of the same date Randle Hardinge had *'a shoppe or house under the town hall'* which is confirmation that an older building was still in use.[9]

Cattle were sold and dealers came from a wide area. By the early seventeenth century the quality of animals attracted drovers from Essex to buy in Whitchurch and in 1644 a black ox purchased there by a Mr Barnes, probably of Whitmore in Staffordshire, was the subject of an argument taken for resolution to his county authorities of the day. He paid four marks for the beast – (4 x 13s-d or £2-13-4, now £2.67) – which sounds expensive, but there was a civil war on at the time![10]

Among the most detailed of the early documents describing the way the stalls were distributed around the town, and what was sold, were manor court papers in 1662 and 1666. A market toll collector complained of the overcrowding of stalls along High Street between *'the market house and the rye market'*. This blocked cart traffic

> 'September 17 Mrs. Whitmore
> It is ordered that the blacke oxe in variance betweene Mr Barnes and Mrs Whitmore, which Mr Barnes pretends he boughte in Whitchurch market shall be delivered to Mrs. Whitmore's custodie, upon her undertakinge that the same oxe shall be forthcomeinge if the same shall be ordered to belonge to Mr Barnes upon his further prooffe of his lawfull buyeinge of him'
>
> '5 November. Barnes
> Whereas by an Order of the 17th. September last 2 It was Ordered that a black Oxe in variance betwixt Mr. Barnes and Mrs. Whitmore should remain in the Custodie of Mrs. Whitmore untill Mr. Barnes should make further proofe. Now forasmuch as it appears unto us from the Comittee at Wem that he the said Mr. Barnes did buy the said Oxe in Whitchurch markett and payd for the same four markes as by proofe made before the said Committee doth appeare. Wee doe therefore thinke fitt and doe order that the said Mrs. Whitmore shall upon sight hereof deliver unto him the said Mr. Barnes the said Oxe or els in default thereof that shee shall then pay unto him the some of foure markes.'
>
> I.Roots & Pennington, *The Committee at Stafford 1643-45* (1957) p180, 202

and put off potential customers who wanted to deal in corn and grain. Several stall-holders were charged with obstruction, one of whom was selling *'garden stuff'*. The manor court went on to redefine the zones in which particular types of goods could be sold. The markers seem to show that barley, first of all, was restricted to a space somewhere around the present Red Lion and, going south down High Street, there followed spaces for French wheat, peas and fitches taken together; thirdly rye; fourthly hemp and linseed, and finally oats which could occupy as much of the lower part of the street as necessary. Widow Rowley's house overlooked the hemp stalls and Pepper Street divided the rye area from that for French wheat, peas and beans. The implication of the toll collector's application for better regulation of the market is that he could collect a charge only from those selling corn and grain (peas and beans included). Apple, bread and carrot sellers amongst others had been elbowing out the grain sellers and were the cause of the traffic problems. Presumably, they threatened the collector's income as well! The new rules do not appear to prevent anything in particular from being brought for sale, but they do suggest that the market was considered to be chiefly for traders in cereals who had priority rights. [11]

A second toll collector levied a tax on animals driven to market. In 1637 this was Jane Nevett, presumably a widow. At that time, George Midcalfe, then a very old man, had the toll on corn and grain. [12] By 1641 Jane had remarried and was noted as *Jane Rhodes late Nevett* with the right to the *'Tole of drovers'*. [13]

Quite probably toll collectors were different from the two individuals named from time to time in manor court records as clerks of the market. Certainly two such officials were named in court documents in the 1720s – for example, Thomas Higginson and John Broomhall in October 1725. These names changed annually as the men in October 1726 were John Downes and Richard Moss. [14]

Retail trading in the market was an interest second only to having a church in which to worship, according to petitioners to the Earl of Bridgewater in May 1718. Something like 140 men put their names to a document sent to thank the earl for his generous assistance in the rebuilding of St. Alkmunds, after the tower dramatically collapsed in July 1711. They added a request that the earl carry through his intention to build a market hall, so important was this to the town's welfare. However, they were concerned that others had already informed the earl that the proposed site was not suitable. On the contrary, so it is now argued. The waste ground proposed for the building was not fifty yards away from the former market house and, if built there, was only likely to be detrimental to those stall holders who insisted on erecting their booths in the street. Many familiar names can be seen on the large sheet they used – J.Figes, John Benyon, Richard Wicksted and George Payne among them. Of those who made marks, Hugh Roe stands out. [15] If the Duke did facilitate any improvement in market premises this must have been under the town hall marked on Grey's map of 1761. No other building was highlighted as a covered market space.

The operation of the market at this time is illustrated by the bye-laws of the manor copied out in 1714 - or at least, this is a record of what should have happened. The clerk of the market was charged with ringing the bell in one half of the year at one o'clock and for the winter part of the year at twelve o'clock. This signified the end of official trading, but not the end of the day. After the bell, buying and selling took place outside market rules. This is clear from the obligation laid upon innkeepers and others *'that shall receive any Graine or Corne into their Houses and suffer the same to be sold there and not cause the same to be first Brought into the propper Markett place for the said Grane before the ringing of the Market Bell'* – under penalty of a fine of ten shillings.

This occasional copying out of rules, it might be argued, was done mostly on those occasions when they were seen to be frequently broken. It was, incidentally, the duty of the collector of tolls on corn, *'as often as Necessary to repair and amend the Pavements of the streets of the said Town the Inhabitants thereof Laying ready Stones and Sand for that purpose before their respective houses according to an Antient Costome.'* It would not be difficult to conclude that, without a covered space for selling perishable foods, and condemned to stand out in all weathers, as the 1718 petitioners reported, and with the possibility that corn was being sold regularly outside the official market (cutting down the income of the toll collector) ultimately leading to a deterioration of the surfaces of the High Street, Green End and Dodington, Whitchurch was in something of an economic trough.[16]

This is not of course the impression derived from the only traveller who can be called in as a witness – Celia Fiennes. She probably came into town in 1698 and stayed at the Crown Inn. She had just had a rather worrying journey in Cheshire and was relieved to meet on the road traders in Whitchurch market. *'It being market day at Whitchurch as I drew near to it in 3 or 4 mile was continually met with some of the market people'* she subsequently wrote in her journal. *'I passed over a little brook a mile before I came to Whitchurch entered me into Shropshire. This is a large market town'*. Her attention was caught more by two gardens than by the level of prosperity or otherwise of the town, such that she made the place seem very attractive. An apothecary's garden, for example, she found full of *'fruits and greens'*, and the garden at the Crown was a delight with lemon trees, a variety of hollies and box, as well as fine flowers, all in a *'little tract of garden ground'*. Such oases for relaxation after a suspected escape from dangerous highwaymen earlier on that Friday stuck in her memory more than any holes in the street, stalls obstructing traffic and irregular market trading.[17]

By the 1820s the reputation of Whitchurch market was claimed as one that had *'long been noted for the abundance and the reasonable price of provisions'*.[18] As it was in a region noted for its excellent Cheshire variety of cheese there could well have been a ready supply of this on the stalls every Friday. It may also be safe to assume that by this date the old market regulations and practices had fully fallen into disuse and that an ever-larger population in the town itself and surrounding district generated a greater demand for food and other consumer goods requiring more stalls as well as permanent shops. Certainly, market day on a Friday attracted the largest number of locals into town. In 1803, when it was necessary to recruit volunteer part-time soldiers, Friday was the best day to catch them for a signature in the enrolment register.[19]

There was no change in the location of stalls in the first part of the nineteenth century. Many were in the street; some - for the sale of cereals - were under the Town Hall as Bagshaw's *Directory* described in 1851.

'THE MARKET HALL, situate in High Street or Market Street, is a spacious building of brick, with stone finishing and supported by stone pillars. Underneath the hall is a spacious area where the corn-market is held. Here the farmers assemble in considerable numbers on the market day, which has a business-like and animated appearance while the market continues'.[20]

Animal sales no doubt increased in parallel with increased retailing of food until, by the 1860s, the town streets were swamped on market days by the detritus of uncontrolled commercial operations. It drove residents beyond the point of total exasperation. A movement for total reform began.

The struggle for market reform 1864-74

For almost nine years from 1864 onwards Whitchurch was spasmodically in an agony of public argument over whether or not it could, and should, afford the cost of a purpose-built new cattle market and covered retail market. The story of events and the interplay of interests is wonderfully revealing about the way the town was governed and the nature of the political process at the start of a new era. For the first time something like democracy came to Whitchurch, a change not entirely unrelated to the recognition nationally that there were urgent social problems requiring solutions.

Some outspoken residents were particularly keen to improve the quality of the local environment and the range of town amenities. In the end, not only were their plans implemented, but a new Town Hall and Assembly Room were added, all opened in 1872. Subsequently, because of the essential commercial requirements of the cattle market, a new road was constructed which did much to alter the whole lay-out of the town and opened the way for further developments in the late Victorian period.

The initial spark for improvement plans came out of a new local government authority in 1860 with powers laid out in an act of Parliament. A nine man Local Board, first elected by ratepayers in March 1861, was charged with responsibility for improving the environment and so regulating the town's affairs as to raise the standard of public health. The Minute Book of the Board shows that in December 1864 at its monthly meeting consideration was given to *'the necessity of having a Smithfield'* and the chairman was instructed to call a public meeting to gather the general opinion of the town.

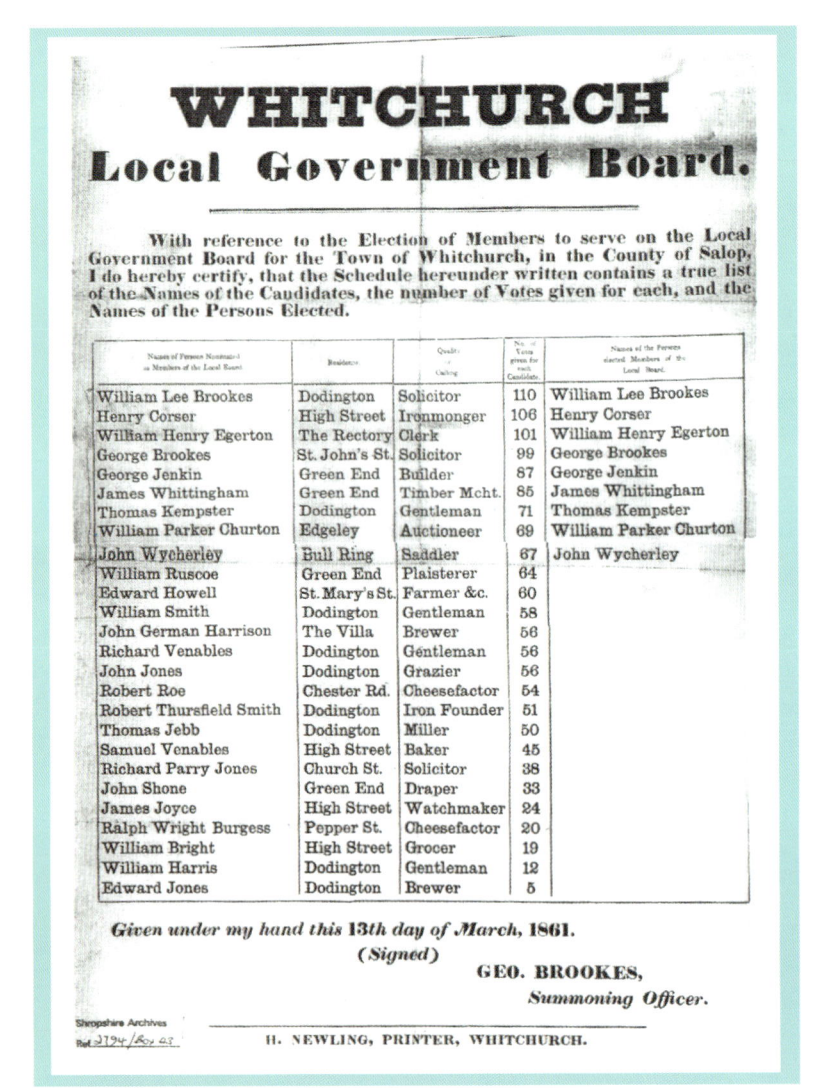

New cattle markets which took the sale of animals out of the principal streets on to specially appointed spaces were now commonly called Smithfields after their more famous

London cousin. Much disease was caused by dirt and decomposing animal and vegetable litter according to popular opinion; herding animals for sale in narrow shopping streets was a practice notoriously productive of piles of noxious waste. Local Board Minute Books tend not to record discussions around issues, but stick to decisions taken and orders given out. It is not possible to be certain about the motivation of the 'reformers' who advocated new market spaces, but the Board was specifically charged with cleaning up and making healthy the streets and buildings in their area. In any case, it seems clear that from the start there wasn't a difficulty persuading people of the need for new market facilities – all arguments concentrated on the problems of acquiring sites, estimating final costs and finding the money to pay for improvements.

Most of the issues surrounding proposals to build a Smithfield and a new market hall were debated in 1865. A public meeting of the inhabitants approved the idea in principle without difficulty. Local Board minutes refer to the necessity of acquiring the rights to a market and thus the income from tolls, and record agreements to start planning and enter negotiations to purchase property. Earl Brownlow was amenable to relinquishing the legal ownership of the market, subject to terms, so potential sites were investigated. Members backed off in June, when part of one potential site was offered for sale, because they felt the Board was not yet in a position to make a bid. [21]

In August 1865 the Board complicated matters further by accepting the need to include an entirely new road in the scheme to allow for easy access to the proposed cattle ground. There was no town newspaper at that stage through the columns of which contemporaries (and later historians) could keep abreast of developments. Just why the process was not only slow, but actually went reverse in February 1866 has to be a matter of guesswork. More than likely the arguments led to the forming of 'parties' and disputes about costs. For the moment, the whole matter was put aside.

In 1867 and 1868 there were desultory revivals of the proposition to build a market hall which centred around the two Churton brothers and their Coach & Horses inn in High Street. One of the Churtons seemed to be suggesting that a public company could be formed to buy his land and build a hall, but it would need Local Board backing to enforce its use. This idea was turned down; it was not to the liking of the Rector, Rev. W.H.Egerton! [22] Monthly minutes in the Board's books record decisions to negotiate, and then the rescinding of orders to that effect, largely determined by the price the Churtons asked for their property. In March 1868 further consideration was dropped. [23] It may well have been in consequence of this that the chairman of the Board, Mr Parry Jones, resigned his office and his seat just before the annual elections in 1869. It was a waste of his time being on the Board, he was reported as saying, because it did nothing and cost over £90 a year for no sufficient purpose. He had been a member for six years and seen nothing worthwhile. [24]

No progress of any kind took place until December 1869. Then the Board again agreed to call a public meeting on Saturday the 4th to test wider local opinion. Earlier in the year - March in fact – Robert Barrow Jones issued the first edition of his newspaper, the *Whitchurch Herald,* and opened a new era in local politics. Now there was a weekly medium in which public debates could be conducted, and it may well have been no coincidence that the paper's appearance was followed by action on the market question. Interestingly, the first issue of *Herald* carried an

WHITCHURCH, SHROPSHIRE.
VALUABLE
Freehold and Copyhold PROPERTY,
IN THE HIGH STREET,
(Formerly the Property of the late Mr. JOHN BRADBURY, Innkeeper and Butcher).

TO BE SOLD BY AUCTION, BY MR. COOPER,

At the COACH AND HORSES INN, High Street, Whitchurch, on TUESDAY, the 7th day of December, 1869, at Four for Five o'clock p.m.

LOT 1.

A COMMODIOUS AND OLD-ESTABLISHED
FREEHOLD INN,
Situate in the High Street, Whitchurch, known as the "COACH AND HORSES," with

FOUR FRONT
SHOPS and a DETACHED DWELLING-HOUSE,
YARD, 4 STABLES, AND OUT-OFFICES,

In the respective occupations of Messrs. John Hough, Robert Gill, George Taylor, George Batho, and Joseph Wilson.
There is good and extensive Cellaring under the Premises.

LOT 2.
A FREEHOLD SHOP,
With convenient DWELLING-HOUSE, being No. 37, in High Street aforesaid, with a Stable and Out-Offices, in the occupation of Mr. Thomas Read and Mr. John Hough.

LOT 3.
A COPYHOLD
DWELLING HOUSE AND SHOP,
Being No. 39, in High Street aforesaid, with a COTTAGE and Yard, in the respective occupations of Mr. T. S. Baker and Mr. J. J. Porter.

LOT 4.
A COPYHOLD
DWELLING-HOUSE AND FRONT SHOP,
Being No. 41, in High Street aforesaid, with Kitchen and Yard, in the occupation of Mr. John J. Porter.

LOT 5.
A COPYHOLD YARD,
With Slaughter-house, Stable, Loose Box, and Gig-house, in the occupation of Mr. Edward Cooper.

The whole of the Property lies together, in the centre of High Street, in Whitchurch aforesaid, and is well situated for business purposes. There is a Pump on the Premises, with an excellent supply of water.

The respective Tenants will shew the lots, and further particulars may be had from Mr. JOSEPH REDDROP, Marsh Farm, of Acton, Nantwich; Messrs. BROOKES AND LEE, Solicitors, or the AUCTIONEER, Whitchurch, Shropshire.

---

item on Wem praising the enterprise of one Mr Franklin, n auctioneer, who *'at very considerable expense, built and fitted up a most convenient Smithfield'* at which he held monthly sales. There was here a strong implication that Wem could soon displace Whitchurch in the market business! [25]

Two things had been decided, in effect, during the four years of delay. One was that new markets were urgently needed; the other was that the best site for a market hall was in High Street and the Coach & Horses had to make way for it. The immediate catalyst was the news in November 1869 that the inn and neighbouring houses were offered for sale at auction. The Churtons, presumably, having failed to get the Board to buy the ancient buildings at their price, forced the issue by going to auction. 'Reformers' hastily drummed up a petition to the Board, signed by 27 principal tradespeople, urging the purchase of the property; the Board called the public meeting to ratify plans to buy, and then sent representatives to the sale of the inn and adjacent buildings where their bids were successful. The total price was £2,230, or £770 below that demanded previously by the Churtons. [26]

The agony was far from over, however. The site was not quite large enough for public rooms and shops, which some thought very desirable. Space for a specialist cheese fair was considered economically advantageous too. In addition, of course, there were still the issues of a cattle market and access roads to both the hall and Smithfield. Room for further argument was created, for instance, by the fact that three men had purchased the Coach and Horses and neighbouring buildings on behalf of the Board, but, for the moment, legally owned the properties in their own right. Conveyance to the Board had still not been completed in July 1870. There were those who took virtual veto on the use of the High Street site for **market purposes.**

Small town politics is brightly illuminated in the columns of the *Whitchurch Herald* as it reported on Local Board meetings. The convoluted debates on property purchases included much detail on price and negotiating tactics. A nice case was that of Dr. Brown and his premises which were another possible route into the market hall. He stood out for something like £1,500 for about a thousand square yards. A long session was spent discussing how far to go in meeting this price, whether it should be pursued at all, what the chance was of getting a compulsory purchase order and at what cost for that. [28] Of course, the motivations of the participants can only be a matter for speculation but the proposal to enhance Whitchurch's economy with a large civic building did create opportunities for individual profit. The Local Board was an arena where conflicts of interest could at least be seen in action even if readers over a century later cannot always tease out just what press reporters were hinting at.

Financing the market hall project was at the heart of most disputes. By the end of 1871 Mr G.Jenkin was pressing for the whole parish to be brought within the Board's control so that the future burden on the rates could be spread wider. He was outvoted. [29] Borrowing money required approval from the government's Local Government Board. An inspector, Mr Morgan, from London, added to the discussions in June 1870 when he recommended variations on the scheme for property acquisitions. [30] In the end, this did not affect granting permission for loans, nor hold up advertising for architects to submit plans. [31] When knowledge of designs for a market hall spread another controversy began, but by this stage there was no stopping the developments in High Street. Business

this as a chance to press for alternative plans, if for no other reason than the difficulty of access from the rear in St. Mary's Street. Associated with this was the unfortunate circumstance that one small yard for sale along with the Coach and Horses had been bought by Mr Parry Jones and promptly leased out. [27] Parry Jones, in effect, had a

The Building News 3 October 1873

This illustration accompanied a short article describing the work of Thomas M Lockwood of Chester as the architect of Whitchurch Town Hall and Market opened in 1872. John Stringer of Sandbach was the builder and the total cost, including all fittings was £6,100. The Local Board had offices on the ground floor facing into High Street, alongside a Corn Market with the General Market and small fish market area behind. On the first floor was a large hall with a dais, and a market inspector had accommodation provided within the complex.

accounts for finding the money show that £5,000 was raised and individual lenders were listed. For example, Miss Jebb of Whitchurch invested £500 and Mr John Cooper also of Whitchurch £400. A surprising amount of the cash, however, came from out of town – Sandbach, Malpas and Liverpool among other places. [32]

There were still minor property disputes between the Board and owners of properties bordering on the new market hall site in January 1871, but tenders were now invited from builders. It had taken over six years of active consideration to get this far. Even so, it was only half the markets project and together they were still only a modest proportion of the concerns of the Local Board. Water supply and sewage were other pressing issues.

The completion of building in October 1872 was the signal for a most amazing event – a visit from the lord of the manor! Earl Brownlow, otherwise known as Sir Adelbert Wellington Brownlow Cust, 3rd Earl Brownlow, with his countess, Adelaide, the daughter of the 18th Earl of Shrewsbury, Henry John Chetwynd-Talbot, came on 6 November to view the new Town and Market Halls and thus effectively open them. It was the first time the earl had been in the town where he had inherited property in 1867. The occasion was marked by highly decorated streets, several triumphal arches over roads into town, peals of bells and crowds lining the earl's route as he progressed up High Street to the new building. Thereafter, he and his party went to St. Alkmund's church and finally the Workhouse. Here, the inmates had a special meal, men had an issue of tobacco and women packets of tea. The Local Board's address of welcome took good care to thank the earl for the gift of the market tolls, but added that a site for new roads and a Smithfield still depended on him agreeing to surrender property. In return, Earl Brownlow promised to give this his urgent attention. [33]

In January 1873 a ball was held in the Assembly Rooms of the new Market Hall to celebrate its opening. With tickets at 10s/6d (52p) this was not for the bulk of the populace! However, from January 1872 monthly cheese fairs were fixed for the third Monday of each month which signalled a new commercial era for the town, it now having retail facilities to match, or even out-do, rival centres such as Nantwich, Wem and Ellesmere, if not quite in the Chester and Shrewsbury league.

Whitchurch 1872 on the last Friday when the market was held in the street in a photograph attributed to J.R.Crosse by T..C.Duggon in his History of Whitchurch (1935)

Left : *The east side of High Street showing the sign board of the Coach and Horses. This must have been taken before 1872 and the demolition of the inn for the new Market Hall. The photograph was attributed to J.R.Crosse by T.C.Duggan in his History of Whitchurch (1935)*

Left below : *The Town Hall in High Street just before or after it was significantly enlarged in 1902 with a gift from E.P.Thompson of Paul's Moss. This added a museum, library and art gallery to the complex.*

Right below: *Testing cheese at Whitchurch Dairy Show 1921 in the Market Hall built in 1872*

Left: *Whitchurch Herald reported the fire which destroyed much of the Town Hall building used as a cinema called the Regent. The Reference Library was also completely burnt out, but museum and art gallery exhibits were saved. Ironically, wartime precautions to prevent lights in rooms from being seen outside contributed to the late discovery of the conflagration.*

Below: *In the mid-1950s the lower floor of the Town Hall and market building were still in use when a parade up High Street brought crowds into town for a celebration. Soon after 1970 the site was cleared and the present Civic Centre erected to provide the town once again with an assembly room and market hall.*

End Notes

1. *Gazetteer of Markets and Fairs to 1516* from internet site for Centre for Metropolitan History
2. Alan Everitt, 'Markets 1500-1640' in J Thirsk edit *Agrarian History of England and Wales* vol. IV, 1967
3. Originally, according to the 1292 Shropshire Assize case, markets were held on Wednesdays – see below.
4. R. W. Eyton, *Antiquities of Shropshire* vol X, Part 1 (1860) p21-23
5. *Calendar Charter Rolls*, 1341–1417, p. 174 cited in *Gazetteer of Markets and Fairs to 1516* (see above)
6. Francesca B.G.Bumpus, *Society, government and power in the Lordship of Blakemere, North Shropshire c1350 – 1420* University College of Wales, Aberystwyth, unpublished PhD 1998
7. ShropsA 212/446/44
8. R. B. James, *Shops and Shopkeepers of Whitchurch* (no date) Pt 1, p5. He doubted that this was anything other than an enlarged stall but did not quote his source. However, there may be some mention of a 'town hall' in a court case held in Chester c1610 which could be confirmation that sheltered market space was still available then.
9. ShropA 212/346 (20/2)
10. P. R. Edwards in Victoria County History of Shropshire vol.4 p 164 using PRO E134/11 Chas I East./20. Also I.Roots & Pennington *The Committee at Stafford* (1957) p180, 202
11. ShropA 212/446/46-49
12. '*A Booke of Informacons of the tenants …*' ShropA 212/Box 346 (20/2))
13. Survey of tenants etc 1641 by Richard Hyde & John Aldersey, page 2, ShropA 12/100.
14. Whitchurch Manor Presentments ShropA 212/48
15. ShropA 212/446/45
16. ShropA 212/59c, Standing orders and byelaws …
17. Celia Fiennes *Through England on a Side Saddle in the Time of William and Mary* (London: Field and Tuer, The Leadenhall Press, 1888) internet version
18. T. Gregory, *The Shropshire Gazetteer* 1824 p705-6
19. Rev. E. Butcher on his way to Chester from Sidmouth (a nonconformist minister), Letter VI dated at Chester on July 25, 1803 in E. Butcher, Excursion from *Sidmouth to Chester in Summer 1803* (1805 London) Brit Lib ref 291.b.39 or G.16074 : *Shrewsbury Chronicle* on 29 July reported that *'books for signature open every day this week 11.00 am to 1.00 pm except Friday when to be opened at Town Hall from 10.00 am to 5.00 pm; and Sunday 24th again at house of Mr John Churton the Par. Clerk'.*
20. S. Bagshaw, *Directory of Shropshire 1851* p342
21. Minute Book of the Local Board ShropA DA15/100/1 27 June 1865 (hereafter LB Minutes)
22. LB Minutes 5 June 1867
23. LB Minutes 4 March 1868
24. *Whitchurch Herald* 1869 March 13 p4 [hereafter Herald]
25. Herald 1869 March 13 p4
26. Herald 11 December 1869 in an editorial.
27. Herald 1870 July 16
28. Herald 1870 July 23
29. Herald 1872 January 6 p6. Jenkin apparently quoted Nantwich as getting a Market Hall for £2,000 because Mr Tollemache gave the site. The Whitchurch hall would cost £12,000, he claimed.
30. LB Minutes 1870 June 15
31. LB Minutes 1870 August 10
32. Local Board Treasurer's Ledger p141, ShropA DA15/300/1
33. Herald 1872 November 9 p4

Land Valuation Maps (1910): Tilstock surveyed

There is a connection, surprisingly, between a report of weekly beer sales in a Tilstock pub on the eve of the First World War and Lloyd George's plan in 1909 to end poverty. At the Horse Shoe the tenant behind the bar was called Burgess. It was a tied house belonging to the Whitchurch Brewery and had four acres of land close by. There were three beers for sale, the cheapest sold at three half pence a pint, another at three and a half pence a pint, and the third sold for two pence a glass. (1p and 2p today). [1]

At least, that was the report an Inland Revenue Department surveyor made in his notebook while doing his rounds in the village about 1913. His job was to get information about the value of land, whether built on or not, in preparation for a tax the Chancellor of the Exchequer, David Lloyd George, had announced in his budget in 1909. At the time, the Treasury wanted money both for the first payment of pensions to the elderly and to pay for six battleships for the Royal Navy. Lloyd George proposed to find this from a tax on increases in land values. He had two wars in mind – the possibility of naval battles with an unnamed enemy, and what he called his 'war on poverty'. These tax plans caused an almighty political row, two general elections in 1910 and significant alterations in the powers of the House of Lords. We can't know what the customers in the public bar at the Horse Shoe made of all this, or what profit R.J.Burgess made out of the £6.00 worth of beer he sold on average every week. The notebooks of the surveyors who plotted every piece of landed property on special maps are available for inspection, and local historians will find this snippet of commercial information deep in the mines of facts awaiting exploitation. [2]

Indeed, this point is worth emphasising. The material information assembled by central government between 1910 and 1915 is not sufficiently explored by family and local historians. One reason for this is that the two principal forms of record are accessible only in the offices of The National Archives at Kew. Some use has already been made in this present book of the maps drawn by surveyors touring Whitchurch town. Their immediate knowledge was of Whitchurch in the Edwardian age and they had much more to say about this period of the town's development than was incorporated into the brief look at the Salisbury Road district, for example, and at the West End. To make best use of their work it is necessary to analyse their notebooks held by The National Archives.

The Horse Shoe pub as seen in 2008

An instance of the value of the Land Valuation maps can be seen in the pattern of farms found in Dodington by the surveyors. This is apparent when a comparison is made between the three farms numbered in their Notebooks as 1230, 1492 and 1527 and those plotted out by Tithe Award mapmakers in 1839, Grey in 1761 and William Fowler in 1651 (pages 88, 73, 48 respectively). Of the several aspects of this comparison which are immediately striking, one is the clear evidence of how farms grew in size as economic pressures and changes in land management techniques in the second half of the nineteenth century forced out the inefficient and the under-resourced holders of a few dozen acres. These three farms, Blackoe, Hadley and Belton were still owned by Earl Brownlow – about 872 acres between them. No doubt, there is some testimony here also to the continuing strength of the aristocratic estate. It is worth noting too how farm boundaries sometimes adjusted to major changes in the landscape, in this case the digging of a canal and the construction of a railway, and sometimes overcame these man-made obstacles to good farming.

By way of contrast, some of the details of property ownership in Whitchurch town are summarised in the map of the New Street - Highgate district. The property boundaries have been copied as the surveyors delineated them, but what is emphasised is part of the pattern of ownership. This shows clearly that in this area George Thomas Johnson had a big interest, possessing the Dairy and associated buildings as well as land stretching east to New Street on which the Urban District Council had a materials store for road maintenance work. This is the kind of information supplied by the valuers in their notebooks in which they named owners and occupiers, gave some description of the buildings and their uses, and recorded the data on which they based their financial calculations. G.T.Johnson, who lived in Chester Road, at The Firs, also owned Havannah Buildings, Havannah House and the cottages in between previously noted (page 12). So, for example, the Dairy itself was tenanted by Richard Sharps. It contained a slaughter house as well as stables and was situated in open fields. Havannah House was at the New Street end of the terrace and was occupied by Alfred Henry Deakin. The surveyors made no comment on the state of the dwellings but all were homes

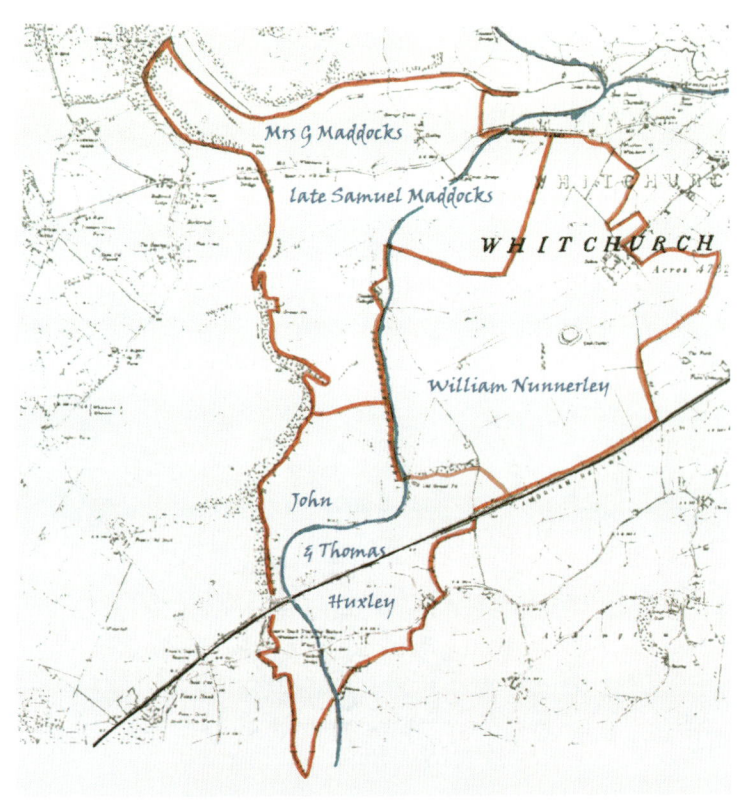

Dodington farms c1912
Farms on the Brownlow estate marked with their occupiers as on the Land Valuation maps

New Street and Highgate area

The land valuers identified properties within the green border as owned by G.T. Johnson and those in the blue border as belonging to Richard Newbrook

to named people. There is plenty of other evidence pointing to these as being amongst the least comfortable and healthy habitations found in Whitchurch at the time.

Interestingly, Richard Newbrook, at No. 1 Wrexham Road, was the one especially noted as having a modern house, brick-built and two storeyed with a yard and stables. There were four bedrooms to share among residents, and a bath as well as living rooms and a kitchen. Newbrook also owned four cottages, right up against his boundary wall, with small gardens, outside WCs in a block and one watertap between them. Fortunately, there was only one resident family. Other aspects of the surveyors' findings, such as Scotland Street houses on the south side divided among different owners – one living in Hull – could be explored. The Highgate Inn's level of sales was not noted, but its bagatelle room was. Perhaps the most obvious point to make, however, is that the canal basin and wharves north of Park Avenue were owned by the Shropshire Union Railway and Canal Company and were not open to further inquiry. Commercial property was subject to special rules.

Tilstock

For another close look at the work of the Land Valuation surveyors, to bring out features of their activity useful for the local historian, it's helpful to look at a different district – hence the focus here on Tilstock.

Tilstock was the only village in the ancient manor of Whitchurch that might have grown into an urban community as a rival to the settlements around St. Alkmund's church. It never did, although it had a chapel from the sixteenth century and eventually a shop or two and artisan workshops loosely gathered around a road junction. In 1851, for example, it had five shops including a grocer and ironmonger, four pubs, two rope makers, a blacksmith, two wheelwrights and a drill-machine man, as well as two tailors, a dressmaker, shoemakers and maltsters. The census of 1841 recorded 136 houses and 637 inhabitants. It was hardly a rapidly growing community – in 1861 the population was 656 and had dropped to 618 by 1911. [3] A turnpike road passed through the village linking Shrewsbury to Whitchurch. The village smithy was strategically sited, opposite the Horse Shoe Inn, in the centre of a junction with a cross-country routeway. On a similar island site, a few yards further north, was the National School built in 1834. Other signs of the importance of Tilstock to its immediate hinterland was a Fire Engine House alongside the Horse Shoe public house and a Post Office opposite the school.

The township contained several large farms. A substantial area on the western side was known as Tilstock Park. This had been a protected area in medieval times reserved, no doubt, for deer hunting the story of which is best kept for another occasion. One of the first two maps for parts of Whitchurch manor, an early seventeenth century mystery already noted, shows the park enclosed and split between three occupiers (see page 55). The pattern of land holding thus created held good until well into the twentieth century. The surveyors in 1913 plotted Upper and Lower Tilstock Park farms and Alkington Farm much as George Grey described them in 1761 – albeit with fields distributed between them in different ways.

Grey's map located leased property only, not copyhold, and this is another way of seeing a difference between the eastern and western parts of Tilstock. The village community lies in the eastern section, largely a copyhold area, still evident as such in 1913, with a large number of relatively small holdings in contrast with the few large farms occupying the western part of the township. Unfortunately, the notebooks do not contain farm plans or descriptions of farmhouses as they do, for example, for Norbury in Staffordshire and Holmes Chapel in Cheshire. It is possible to list occupiers and to identify the owners so that, for example, the residual estate of the Bridgewaters, held by Earl Brownlow by the second half of the nineteenth century, is recognisable. The Brownlow properties were Lower Tilstock Farm, Upper Tilstock Farm otherwise known as Massey House Farm, and Alkington Farm. In 1920 much of the Brownlow estate was sold, including Lower Tilstock. It was then 160 acres in extent, as it had been before 1914, and the sale catalogue described the farmstead as a "superior house ... constructed of brick and slate, contains Dining Room, Drawing Room, House Place, Office, 4 Bedrooms, Box Room, Kitchen, Scullery, Cellar and 2 Dairies, whilst approached by a secondary stairway there is a Man's Room and a Cheese Room." Nothing unusual, in other words, for a farm of moderate size on an aristocratic estate. [4]

Right: *The principal farms as plotted by the Land Valuation surveyors about 1912 with the names of occupiers. Maddocks, Dudleston and Batho were tenants of Earl Brownlow, but Edwin Chase was a tenant on the lands of the trustees of John Thursfield.*

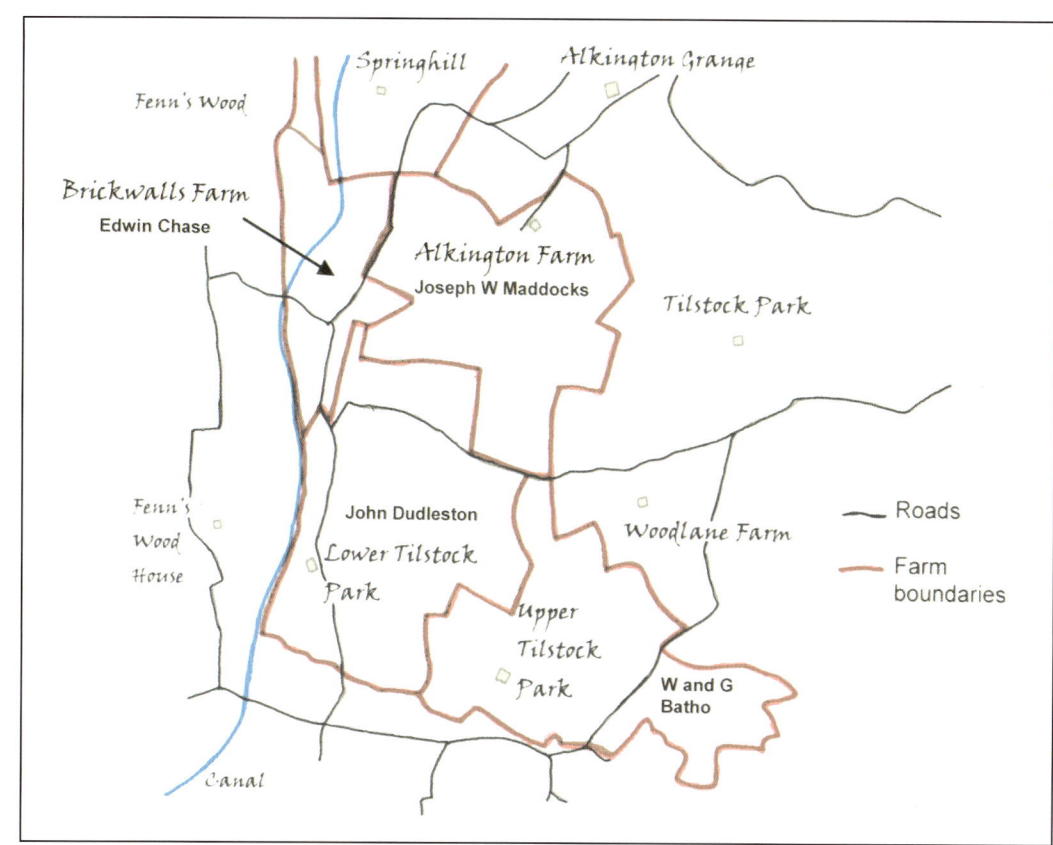

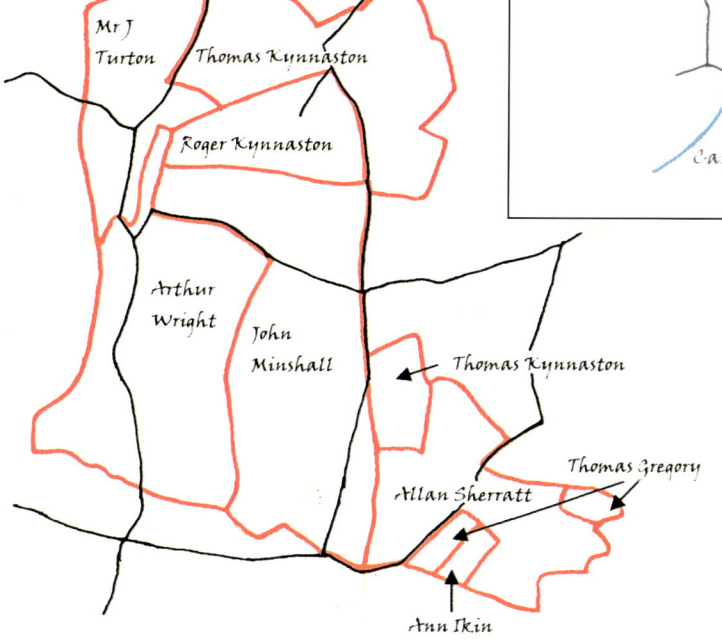

Left: *The principal farms in the Tilstock Park area of Tilstock township are shown as recorded by George Grey in 1761. Eight tenants then occupied this part of the Bridgewater estate. The land they held closely corresponded with the area divided between three tenants named on the plan dated about 1600 (see page 55).*

Tilstock township was chiefly characterised by this diversity of farm holdings and owners throughout the second half of the nineteenth and in the twentieth centuries. It was an open rather than a closed community – indeed, this may have been the case in earlier ages despite the lordship of the earls and dukes of Bridgewater. In 1851 Bagshaw, in his *Directory of Shropshire,* noted George Corser, John Goodall, Francis J. Hughes, John Whitfield and Mrs Wood among the landowners, as well as mentioning the presence of a number of other, unnamed, freeholders. In 1871 another Directory claimed that the chief landowners were Viscount Hill and George Sandford Corser. [5] In 1913 it was considered that W. St. John Hazeldine of Shrewsbury and the trustees of the late Mrs Wood, also of Shrewsbury, owned the largest share of the land. [6] This last assertion can be well tested by analysing the findings of the agents for the land tax survey touring the area in 1913.

This section of one of the maps as drawn by the Land Valuers shows how they carefully registered the boundaries of every separate property. Steel Heath is on the eastern side of Tilstock and the patchwork of small holdings is well demonstrated

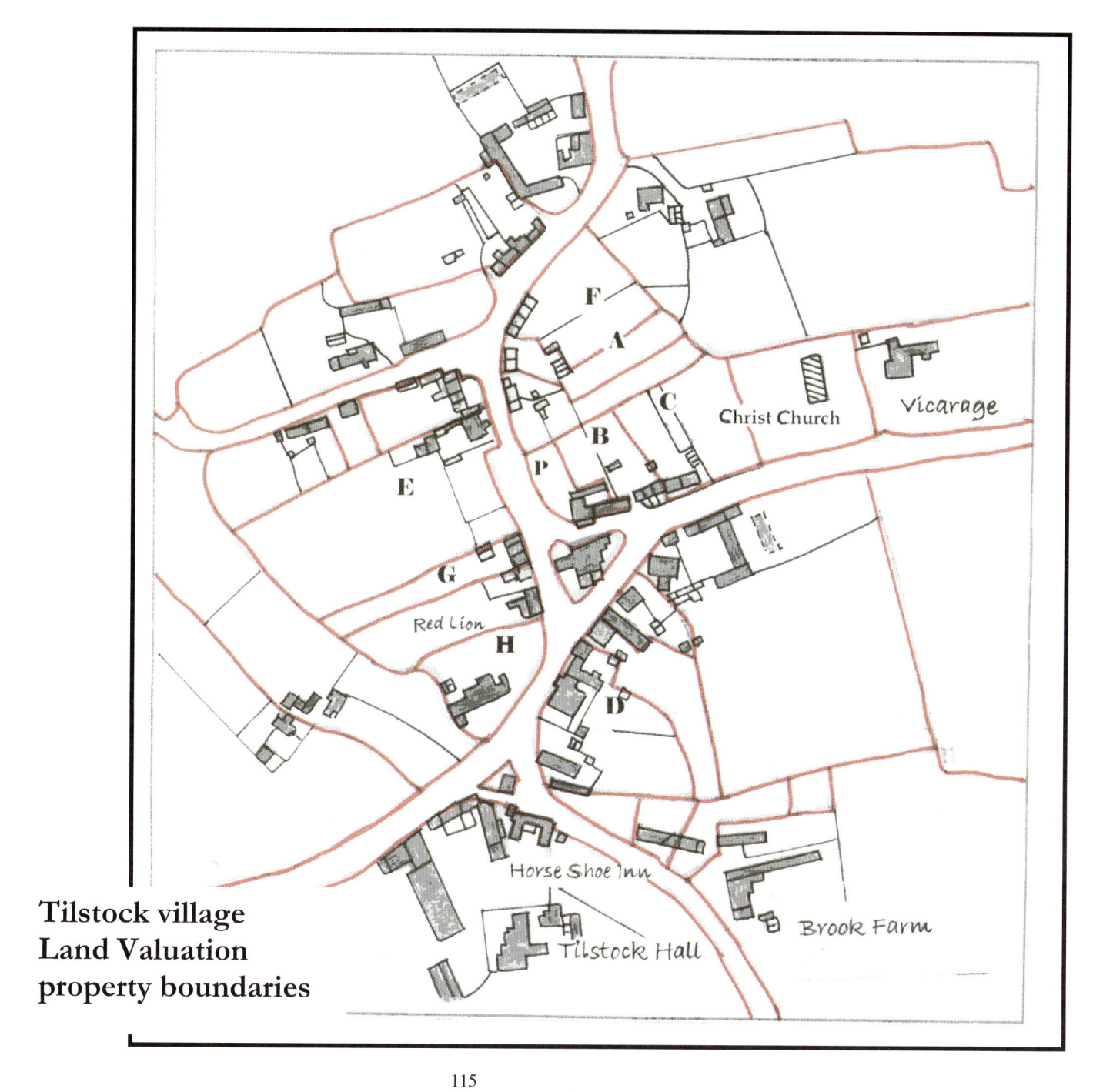

**Tilstock village
Land Valuation
property boundaries**

The village surveyed

Land Tax surveyors measured land and made financial calculations to fix a base value to property from which it was intended at some future date to work out what increase had taken place on which to levy a tax. The intention was never carried out, but the maps and Field Note Books recording all the information provide a snapshot of Tilstock as it was on the eve of the First World War. Only a few sketchy drawings were made in the Notebooks, no doubt to serve as aids to the memories of the men who subsequently drew the master maps. They show the layout of a number of dwellings around the road junctions. Surveyors finally plotted the boundaries of all pieces of property in bold red lines on Ordnance Survey maps. Their pencil sketches are here redrawn to elaborate an outline plan of the village, and the information in the notebooks is summarised in a narrative explanation.

When visitors came into the village from the south they found Brook Farm on the east side of the road from Shrewsbury and Tilstock Hall Farm on the west side. Brook Farm was tenanted by Robert Ellison and owned by George Batho who lived in Whitchurch. At 28 acres and a yearly tenancy this was a modest holding and had recently been reduced when nine acres of detached ground had been sold for £475. Tilstock Hall, on the other hand, was the largest farm to adjoin the village being some 201 acres in extent. It had belonged to George Sandford Corser and was occupied by John Horton when the surveyor called. Horton came into this in 1895 and, apparently, paid a rent of £346 per annum. Immediately next to the hall there was The Horse Shoe pub already noted, and across the narrow street, where a road came in from the west, and in the very centre of the junction in an

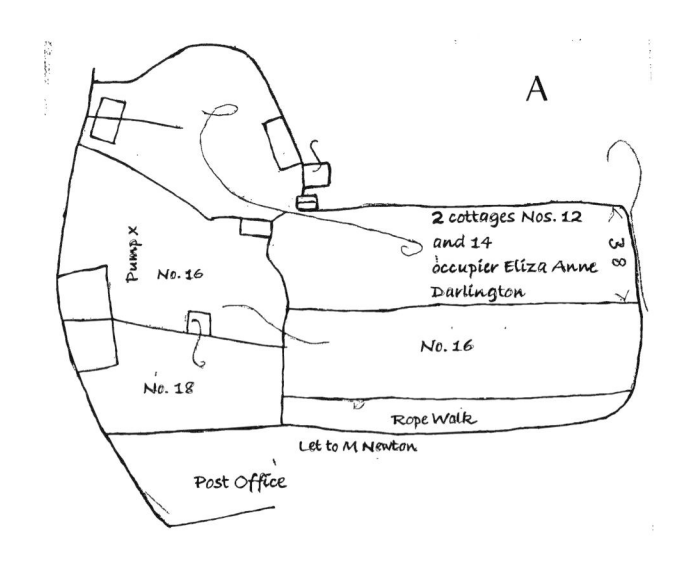

Four pencil sketches found in the notebooks

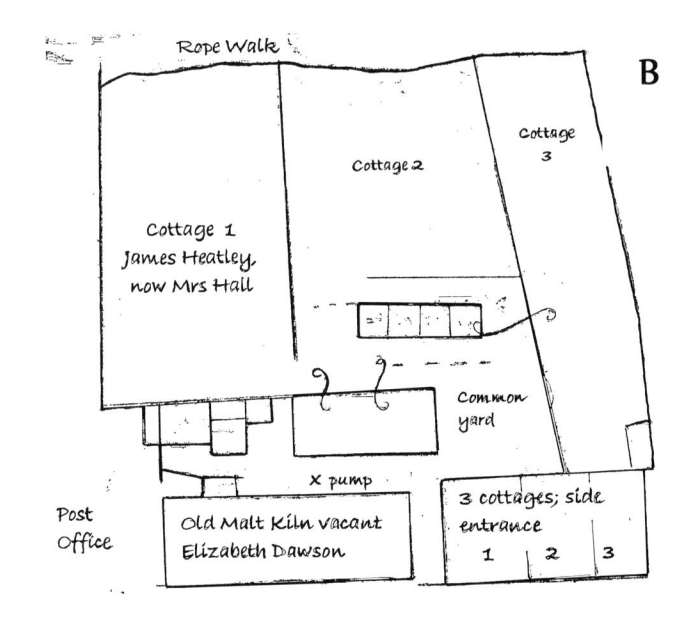

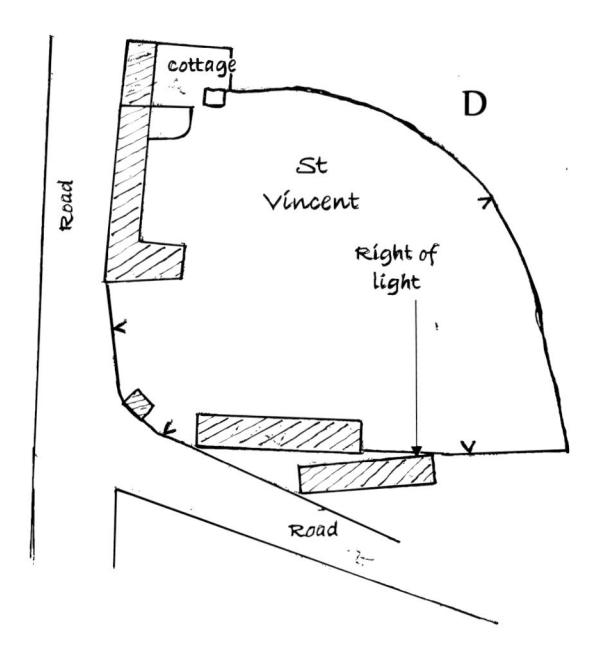

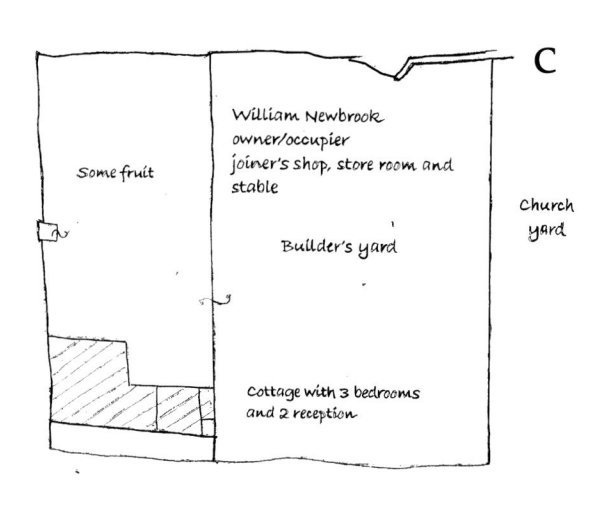

island building, was the village smithy. William Barnet Dudley ran this and the ownership lay within his own family. Just beyond this junction, on the east side was a house called St. Vincent. Alice Evelyn Jervis owned and occupied this largish property which had four bedrooms, two attics, a bath, three reception rooms and a cellar (site D on the sketch and village map). It had fetched a good price when for sale in September 1906 -- £650 according to the valuer. He was sufficiently puzzled by the layout that he made a quick sketch plan in his book, but one rather short on detail! He didn't say either what sort of improvements had been made recently which cost £170. Directly opposite was Rosebank where James Bridge lived (site H on the village map). He had acquired this in 1910 for £600 and he had since that time spent £200 on improvements.

The three central village institutions were found by the surveyor a little further north along the street at the cross roads where the school occupied the middle position. To the west or left hand side was the Red Lion, and north of the school was the Post Office. Here again the surveyor needed an aide-mémoire as support for later map making, and he made three quick pencil drawings of buildings and boundaries. At the very least, they demonstrate the difficulties faced by agents whose job it was to sort out and define rights, and their financial value, in an ancient village with customs and conventions well known to the locals more by word of mouth than by written record. Among the particularly serious concerns was access to water. The surveyors in Tilstock made careful note of who could use which pump and at what charge. Mains water had yet to solve an ancient problem of an adequate supply of safe water.

References on these sketch maps to a rope walk, an old malt kiln, a joiner's shop and a builder's yard help a parish historian pin down just where local businesses operated, or, at least, had once been sited. The valuer who walked around Tilstock added some detail in his notebook also worth comment. The rope walk (site A on the village map) was owned by Mrs Elizabeth Griffiths who lived in Bootle, Lancashire. The main dwelling and the adjacent pair of semi-detached cottages had been bought a few years previously for £250 and another £250 had been spent on rebuilding part or all. William Newbrook's Beach Cottage (probably the writer meant Beech) with his storeroom, joiner's workshop, stable and builder's yard had been sold in September 1901 for £150 and some £110 had been spent since on improvements and drains. He had three bedrooms and two living rooms in his house (site C). In the first of the three cottages alongside the vacant former malt kiln, James Heatley had been replaced by Mrs Hall. These cottages had tiny gardens behind a common yard and the point of putting the pump site on the plan was that this was the one shared between the occupants (see site B on the village map).

The store of information about Tilstock properties shows variety rather than consistency. Another owner who lived out of the village was Miss Alice Hayes of Wrexham Road, Whitchurch (see site F). She had four cottages let at a weekly rent amounting to £5-10-6 each a year. Alfred Norton ran the shop (see site E) just north of the Red Lion pub, but his premises were owned by William Knowles of Bolton in Lancashire. Norton's immediate neighbour (site G) was Joseph Batho who lived in two of the three half-timbered and brick cottages noted by the valuer as 'old'. In 1890 this property had been sold for £160. Unfortunately for the village historian there was little written down about the schoolhouse where the resident was T.W. Jones, or the house, garden and croft occupied by John Prince. In fact, this area appears to have been surveyed somewhat late in the Inland Revenue process of valuing land when some of the regulations on what had to go into notebooks had been relaxed.

Despite the lack of consistency in the survey of Tilstock there is much for the historian to garner, and great value in having evidence about the village at one point in time. The only previous attempt at a complete listing of properties, owners and occupiers, with plans of their individual boundaries, was the 1830s Tithe Award. Nothing earlier has been found and nothing later is an equivalent. It is, of course, also somewhat frustrating now to fall short of a full account of Edwardian Tilstock based on the Land Valuation maps and Notebooks. A village historian has plenty to do to develop this brief study, especially if it can be linked to the 1901 census records, commercial directories, newspaper items and such ephemera as parish magazines and sale posters. There is a feeling that by the time of the First World War – perhaps a little earlier – Tilstock and Whitchurch no longer recognised their common history as parts of the manor of Whitchurch. Earl Brownlow still owned farms in Tilstock, however, though they were soon disposed of when the war ended. That then was the final separation.

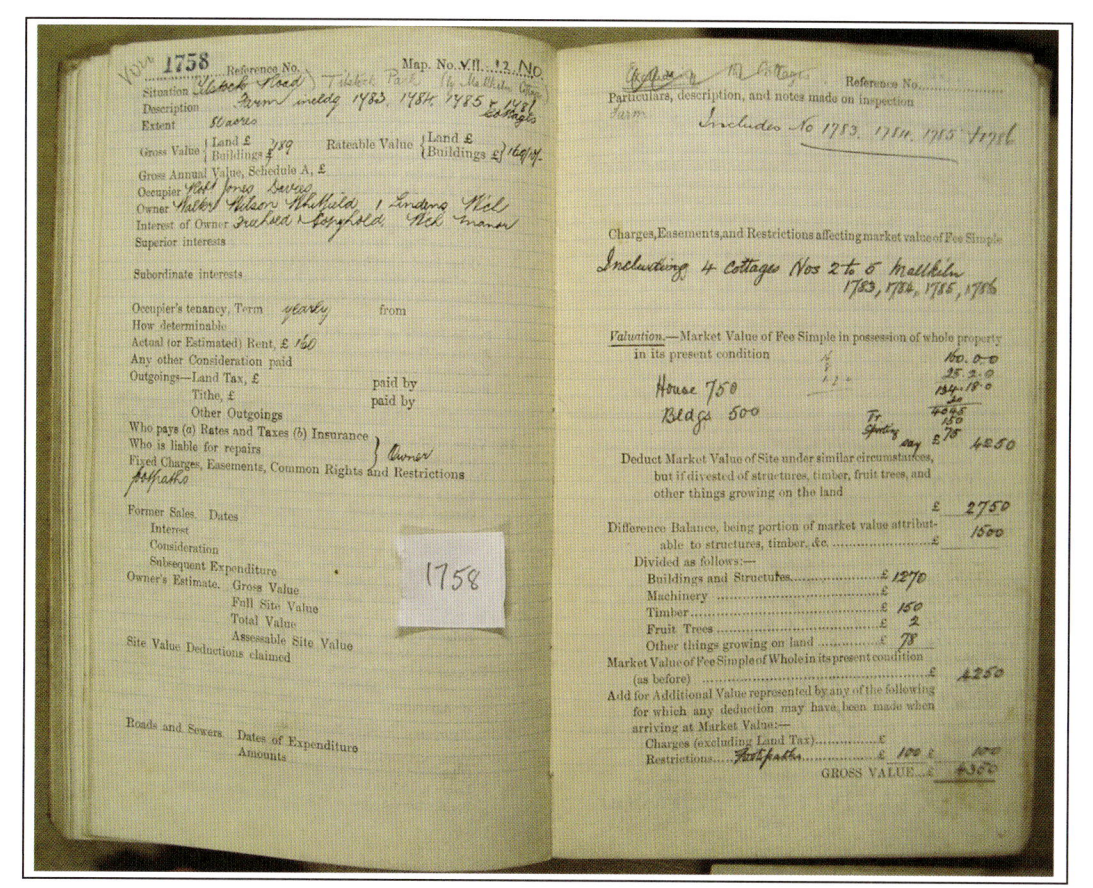

Two of the four pages in a Field Notebook devoted to each property, in this case Tilstock Park Farm number 1758. The occupier was Robert Jones Davies who also held four cottages numbered 1783, 1784, 1785 and 1786

End Notes

1. This section is based upon Land Valuation records kept at The National Archives at Kew (TNA) and associated documents lodged in the Shropshire Archives in Shrewsbury.

2. All the information and maps from the Land Tax Survey has been gathered from TNA IR58/76059 to 76091 which are the Field Note books arranged in successive blocks of 100 properties; and IR132/4/38 to /4/47 which are the maps. Shropshire Archives 4011/93/1,2,3 : 4044/100 are references to the Valuation Books not collected in by TNA. These summarise the financial calculations, and the properties run sequentially from number 1 onwards. The County Record Office also holds some of the working maps used by the surveyors.

3. S. Bagshaw, *Directory of Shropshire 1851* p362 : E. Cassey & Co., *Directory of Shropshire 1871* : Kelly's *Directory of Hereford and Shropshire 1913*

4. Sale Catalogue for Bridgewater Estate February 1920

5. E. Cassey & Co., *Directory of Shropshire 1871*

6. Kelley's *Directory of Herefordshire and Shropshire 1913*

119

Last thought – a look towards the future

This is the end of only one exploration. It has brought up more questions than it has answered about that 'past country' we call History. There has been a deliberate selection of ways into the story of how Whitchurch has evolved over the four hundred years since Sir Thomas Egerton bought the manor in 1598. It is inevitable that this has happened because there are so many different routes the historical explorer can travel that no one can go down them all – certainly not all at once. If that is irritating and unsatisfactory, that too cannot be escaped. The past is huge, the present far too brief to allow all to be revealed. However, everyone who has reached this far can now go further, by branching out from the evidence already investigated in part, or starting afresh with different documents, field and hedgerow studies, photographs, oral accounts of lives, Club committee minutes and newspapers just as a few examples.

One thing is very evident from encounters with clues about the past in Whitchurch and that is that it is now, and always has been, an artificial construction. Town, manor, parish, township and urban district have been used at different times to indicate some kind of unity, some kind of community; a geographical space within which human activity has been focussed, distinct from similar neighbouring entities. A sense of belonging to this particular place, with all its penumbra of historical traditions, social characteristics and physical remnants of past times, is what really defines Whitchurch. This is a psychological condition, not a geographical or administrative determinant. Historians know this, but can't easily describe how people over many hundreds of years have felt at home here. For the most part, historians only have the clues left in papers substantially created by officials of a multitude of governing bodies. Occasionally, there are private business records and a few collections of family and individual ephemera, plus, of course, the artefacts preserved in museums, the built environment of streets and alleyways, with the features of surrounding landscapes so tellingly revealing about the past to those with the eyes to see.

Most of the districts within the historical space allocated to Whitchurch have been touched on at some point. Streets and housing estates within the urban area, Black Park, Bubney, Blackoe and Tilstock have been given some attention. There are regrettable omissions such as the two Ashes and the Woodhouses, Edgeley and Broughall: Hinton has been ignored and Hollyhurst and Chinnel too. Future local historians will find other themes more rewarding, such as businesses of all kinds whether manufacturing iron work and clocks, or running hotels and retailing textile fabrics and ironmongery. Firms of solicitors based in the town could be particularly attractive subjects to pursue for they had key roles in so many public institutions, as well as conducting property transfers, arranging mortgages and acting as agents for clients in personal difficulties of all manner of kinds. The role of the churches in the cultural and educational aspects of Whitchurch society is another subject well deserving of detailed investigation, providing building alterations are put aside and the personalities and special interests of clergy and ministers, teachers, musicians and charity organisers are made the centre of attention. There is still a lot to be said about the Local Board and its successor, the Urban District Council. Those who sat on these administrative bodies had numerous social and economic issues to deal with; the manner in which they arrived at policies can still provide us with lessons, if only because many of the environmental, health, educational and social matters are of perpetual significance.

English communities have evolved as entities with their own peculiar characteristics, all the while sharing features of national development. Local historians have a wide country to explore as they venture into the past, and the wisest of them find as many maps as they can to help guide their steps. Some of the more obvious ones have been the subject of this book.